Penguin Books

The *Daily Telegraph*
12th Crossword Puzzle Book

The *Daily Telegraph* 12th Crossword Puzzle Book

Penguin Books

Penguin Books Ltd, Harmondsworth, Middlesex, England
Viking Penguin Inc., 40 West 23rd Street, New York, New York 10010, U.S.A.
Penguin Books Australia Ltd, Ringwood, Victoria, Australia
Penguin Books Canada Ltd, 2801 John Street, Markham, Ontario, Canada L3R 1B4
Penguin Books (N.Z.) Ltd, 182–190 Wairau Road, Auckland 10, New Zealand

Published in book form by Penguin Books 1975
Reprinted 1976, 1977, 1978, 1980, 1981, 1983 (twice), 1985

Printed and bound in Great Britain by
Cox & Wyman Ltd, Reading
Set in Monotype Times

The Puzzles

1

Across

1 A French-Canadian no more than a bit unsettled (8)
5 Enough to make a lapwing cry (6)
9 Clear as a document (8)
10 As plinth it supports, disregarding exclamation (6)
11 Wreathed poet (8)
12 In Spain a large number upset the papal court (6)
14 Defend the right to down tools again? (6, 4)
18 Fifty closely garbed, sensualists all (10)
22 For the equivalent of 5p a go, planetarium visitors may view it (6)
23 Sound proving fatal to Mr Toad? (8)
24 Where a couple of ducks swallow wine (6)
25 Indifferent, I fish around back in the lake (8)
26 Captivating, thanks to a royal following (6)
27 About three ways a Scots regiment reveals age? (8)

Down

1 Unpretentious association with Sir Alec? (6)
2 One spirit Macbeth couldn't stomach (6)
3 Miss Muffet's sit-upon (6)
4 Total noise shattering as the traffic piles up (4, 2, 4)
6 Married in the old-fashioned way (8)
7 What, about an inch? Yet enough for one winger, and . . . (8)
8 . . . more, when one joins others (8)
13 Pop the question? No, the answer (6, 4)
15 Youngster tired of grousing? (8)
16 Blow that wasn't landed, maybe! (4, 4)
17 Chairman with a heart-broken son around (8)
19 & 20 The 1 down ring, relatively speaking (6, 6)
21 Way out for a black girl losing her head (6)

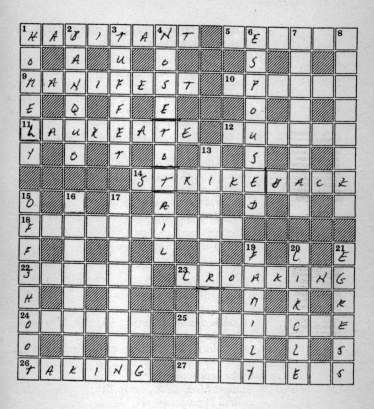

2

Across

1 A function at which steps are taken to relieve distress (7, 4)
8 She daren't change into a new beret (11)
11 The responsibility from which 14 down used to run (4)
12 Lamb and beer brought back about one (4)
13 Scholarly mates? (7)
15 Surprised reaction of a Scot surrounded by French cheese and sponge cake! (7)
16 Specifies other means (5)
17 Sounds as though we have time (4)
18 District from 8 down (4)
19 A flier of epic achievement (5)
21 Spruce market in Japanese currency (7)
22 Noble disturbance about an Arab country (7)
23 It entitles a holding of a boy back (4)
26 I am a swindler revered by the devout (4)
27 In their professional capacity they have lots to offer (11)
28 Need for place in finest holiday region in West Germany (5, 6)

Down

2 When he's around one gets a move on (4)
3 Not fit to trace a reference to its source? (3, 4)
4 An act that makes a change of course (4)
5 There's always a demand for their products in wet countries (7)
6 His works are sung in many a holy temple (4)
7 A shrill and unmannerly masculine calling (4-7)
8 A hill town where traffic is restricted? (5-2, 4)
9 Technological study of current developments (11)
10 It threatens us with violence, naturally (4, 7)
14 One of our forebears from Naxos (5)
15 The joiner may set off with it (5)
19 Sort of patch that is liverish (7)
20 A Russian buck? (3, 4)
24 'Faultily faultless, icily regular, splendidly — ' (Tennyson: Maud) (4)
25 Do nothing but make bread? (4)

26 Olympic runner of eternal fame (4)

3

Across

7 Restrain one's ardour to complete the sketch of a single bull (4, 2, 4, 5)
8 What the crowds do when contestants in T.T. races crash (7)
10 Not all right in a dose of medicine (7)
11 Check sound instrument over (5)
12 Well-educated boy as craftsman (5)
14 It is indivisible; that is most important (5)
15 Notice how to make one's name (4)
16 Grip for carrying large quantities of merchandise (4)
17 Give away, where normally things are sold (4)
19 Is in possession of soft length of yarn (4)
21 Stone-breaking assault (5)
22 Monstrous woman gives a heavenly player the penultimate letter (5)
23 He steers one into a scheme (5)
25 Sporting official who waits on board (7)
26 About fifty sticky substances may be used by an artist (7)
27 What a bold swindler pulls out of the hat? (10, 5)

Down

1 Off-putting, isn't it? (15)
2 Whether added or multiplied, they come to the same (3, 4)
3 Foreign articles below (5)
4 Course . . . (5)
5 . . . confused a rising doctor giving a prescription to keep him away (7)
6 Depict only women formulating insurance (9, 6)
9 Guide that puts the pressure on a bit (4)
10 What the unambitious motorist needs if out of petrol (4)
13 Time when the spirit rises and high tension follows (5)
14 Positive identification on hit material (5)
17 Catch not a single mermaid? (3-4)
18 I'd support father. That's settled (4)
19 One ring never never around two rings (4)
20 Model to talk glibly on a point (7)
23 Cromwellian arrogance (5)

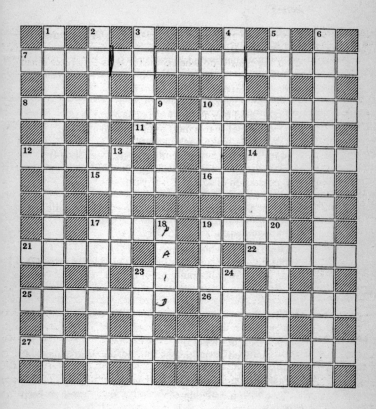

24 Stories of a vital escape (5)

4

Across

1 Impressive representation of the heights to which men may rise (7, 3)
6 Iron-bound engineers set at liberty (4)
10 Covered with gluey material I'm shown the way around (5)
11 Top gear? What a stupid assumption! (6, 3)
12 Last auditor caught in freak storm (8)
13 To resume steady work seems the answer (5)
15 A prospect denied to the underground man? (7)
17 Its bearer commands unusual respect (7)
19 A girl turned ten in neat array (7)
21 The priest is more likely than the soldier to find it relaxing (7)
22 The country from which I learn (5)
24 It offers varied penalties (8)
27 The sort of name our editor is in love with (9)
28 Minor runner put right into reserve (5)
29 Stops for race-drivers, industrially exploited (4)
30 A seer not normally spent out, but in the main monstrous (3-7)

Down

1 An affection marked by its absence? (4)
2 Almost the last man to take over for the Prime Minister! (6, 3)
3 The sequence of command (5)
4 Untidy bed in a castle replete with noble names, perhaps! (3-4)
5 Anne's grabbing at dues that once went to the Pope (7)
7 One who steps up to present a short synopsis (5)
8 Forms to be filled by victors at by-elections (5, 5)
9 Beast went out to follow a sinister trend (4, 4)
14 Travel bargain offer? (5, 5)
16 The rich girl's penniless suitor doubtless counts this promptly! (2, 3, 3)
18 No longer new to adult responsibilities, or possibly not yet new (6-3)
20 See that something is done (7)

21 A screen usually of wood design or reeds (7)
23 Unsuitable in a pot lacking nothing (5)
25 A sea-fowl still warm, though dying (5)
26 Satirical sketch made with 5p outfit (4)

5

Across

1 The poet who produced romance beside fine material (8)
5 Plain as following a parental politician (6)
9 Drain for a dirty smoker? (4-4)
10 Not wholly employed on the stage it would seem (2, 4)
11 Looking amazed (4-4)
12 One who declares obsolete currency (6)
14 Get heating preparations in hand for a Chinese meal (10)
18 Treat wader disposed to get out of his depth? (5, 5)
22 Glossy finish provided by name in Spanish article (6)
23 Add it on, and divide by one – that is what it amounts to (8)
24 The Frenchman pointed his pistol – successfully! (6)
25 Airs once composed for a film plot (8)
26 Give, even though the fellow has had a meal (6)
27 He values a vessel with an arrangement of roses (8)

Down

1 Maybe television is not so much used for it in school (6)
2 Concealed from the reserve I led (6)
3 Now invalid pleads out of order (6)
4 Snake on the obverse of an old penny (10)
6 Not a neat revision to make notes upon (8)
7 Custom legislation included in the cost of the goods (8)
8 Artist is to become a writer (8)
13 Add final courses to be found at the back of the book (10)
15 Mastered in order to be assigned to a certain class (8)
16 Telling one of the family (8)
17 He believes in sticking (8)
19 Betrothed one takes the place of the king in France (6)
20 High hats set at an angle (6)
21 Presumably an entrance within walls (6)

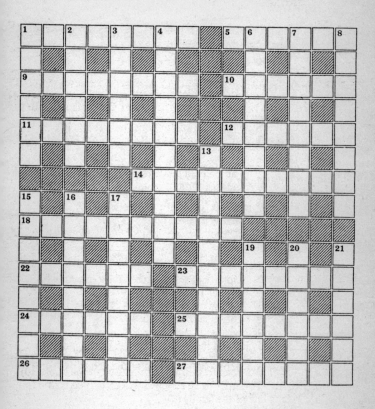

6

Across

1 Suitable home for a boxer's press-cuttings? (5-4)
8 A task that requires to be done over and over again (10, 3)
11 The lot of a teacher, to some extent (4)
12 Calls made with wry grins (5)
13 Outmoded divinity course at Oxford (4)
16 A mould that poses a problem for stage management (7)
17 Ardour displayed in a Victorian book cover (7)
18 Ebullient saint taking international help round (7)
20 'All — ranks the same with God' (Browning: *Pippa Passes*) (7)
21 Capital location for consumers of exotic tastes (4)
22 Odd sort of pleasure-boat (5)
23 Dramatic take-off (4)
26 His working life is full of ups and downs (4, 9)
27 Tradesmen freshly spruced up (9)

Down

2 A group of fellow-craftsmen (4)
3 Continual uproar in a great environment (7)
4 A poet provides the connection that is needed, apparently (7)
5 A cipher-writer ready to do business? (4)
6 Recognised seat for oral examinations (8, 5)
7 Vague philosophy characteristic of the permissive society? (5, 8)
9 Misdirected dish no longer available (3, 6)
10 A girl guide at the theatre (9)
14 Medical man investing in a foreign currency (5)
15 A coffee-bean put in by mistake (5)
19 He's not sure, but changes when the actor goes out (7)
20 Genuine screen I reconstructed (7)
24 Staunch, though far from stern (4)
25 Marginal advantage (4)

7

Across

1 Chisellers employed on relief projects (9)
9 Drive madly, yet always behind a vehicle (6)
10 Head teacher who creates interest (9)
11 A striker from a street in London and in France (6)
12 I object to sort of anger that is displayed by circus owners (9)
13 Guevara hesitates for applause (6)
17 Extra clue to where the abecedarian should seek F (3)
19 Complaint made by second graduate leaving Malabar with a first class return (7)
20 Following sappers about to join up heading back (7)
21 Presumably it prints only worthless material (3)
23 Tacked on invitation to a thirsty dog (6)
27 It is the middle part that bores (6-3)
28 The teetotaller in a trunk is unlikely to be found on it (6)
29 Breach of promise action? (5, 4)
30 Avoid some of the females chewing gum (6)
31 Many machines involve it (9)

Down

2 Opera for motorists (6)
3 In France born liar goes around in anything but circles (6)
4 Dogged like a dog (6)
5 It early developed into actual fact (7)
6 It provides an easy let down for the drop-outs (9)
7 For the best motives the reference was to a source of water (4-5)
8 Objected because publicity man conducted a survey (9)
14 Perhaps a pony is a matter of no consequence (5, 4)
15 Farcical alternatives for that unspoilt child? (9)
16 What suborners do for patient attendants (9)
17 A second gong where one expects time to be heard (3)
18 It comes into energy (3)
22 Nail varnish of one shade (7)
24 The stiffness of man of honour accustomed to the limelight (6)
25 High churchman holds company a low one (6)

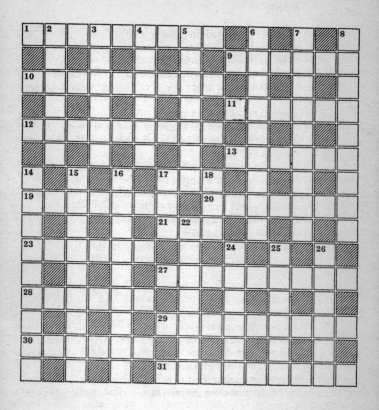

26 They are single failures (6)

8

Across

1 Early fratricide's place of exile – for the rest of his life? (3, 4, 2, 3)
8 A barrage worker, reputedly unyielding (7)
9 Revised caption for a Michigan city or a Redskin conspirator (7)
11 Star-bound measure of heavenly bodies (7)
12 Leaves got up from bed (3-4)
13 Salute with tears in Scotland (5)
14 Ship's follower hung around the ancient sailor (9)
16 Unrivalled yet unmarried? (9)
19 Fabulous moralist takes a retrospective pose (5)
21 Modern entrance for old prison (7)
23 Account for former manifest (7)
24 Longed for 12 months to end in confusion (7)
25 Inner material for a romantic language (7)
26 Statesman to be sat upon in Derbyshire (12)

Down

1 A bar for swinging, daring, youth! (7)
2 Distinction shouldered by an officer (7)
3 Dispute sound suggestion to make a shrewish change (9)
4 Incongruously opted for military H.Q. (5)
5 Sweet, affectionate creature from 8 across (7)
6 South American flower, otherwise in love, commander! (7)
7 Fare of those corridors of power? (7-5)
10 Ruy Lopez, perhaps, institutes action on board (5, 7)
15 Low type of work by a professional chiseller (3-6)
17 Water-side route for those who draw (7)
18 The laughing stock of the African veldt? (7)
19 Conciliatory advice for a very quiet relaxation (7)
20 Deep-living high-flyer (3-4)
22 A water-spin sounds to be his style (5)

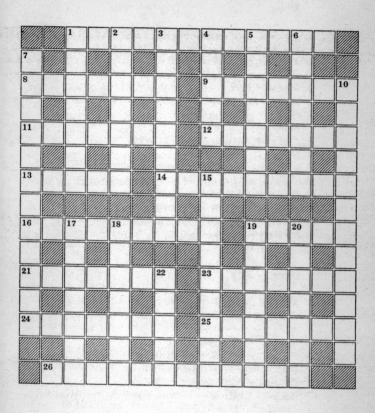

9

Across

6 A request for belief that gets government backing (5, 8)
8 Early pilgrim American playwright (6)
9 Yields from TV shares (8)
10 A well-endowed health centre (3)
11 A book Kipling wrote on love, it may be loosely assumed (6)
12 Carefully going through a South American country to make notes? (8)
14 I get at a review and cause a stir (7)
16 Emerge from the ranks and make speedy progress (4, 3)
20 Savage measures that lead to open conflict (3-5)
23 They get fired. loyal and generous though they are (6)
24 One way to fix a match, maybe (3)
25 Hors d'oeuvres for officials of course? (8)
26 'All is but toys; — and grace is dead' (*Macbeth*, Act 2) (6)
27 An account of what actually happened (4-4, 5)

Down

1 A postal packet that goes overseas (4-4)
2 Confirms what visitors like to see on the Mappin Terrace (5, 3)
3 Non-committal reply to a proposal (7)
4 An article that will certainly be looked into (6)
5 Their main work is done when they go to bed (6)
6 A qualified craft instructor (7-6)
7 Being no obstacle to fortune, nor one of its favourites, apparently (3, 2, 5, 3)
13 The river held back by 12 across (3)
15 She's something of a daring girl (3)
17 Protuberant circus figure entering the Underground (8)
18 Bent ingot panned on the coast of Devon (8)
19 Enhances the appearance of leaves on a journey? (4, 3)
21 Type of fin seen in cod or salmon (6)
22 One ill adapted to ornamental engraving (6)

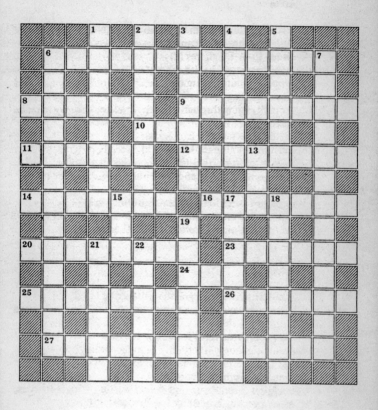

10

Across

1 It is instrumental in renewing an old mine (9)
8 Getting the directors' reactions is a means of increasing the volume (8-5)
11 9 — 1 + 0 = ? There's nothing to it! (4)
12 Right angle in food – and water! (5)
13 Sounds like a drink for the circus star (4)
16 Was once, but no longer is an unruly adolescent (7)
17 Fascist leader surrounded by some in France draws a conclusion (7)
18 Fired an underweight journalist (7)
20 Ship's captain who misses certain booked passages (7)
21 Light gas manufactured from 11 across (4)
22 Clever dandy (5)
23 Period in which devoted man has little work (4)
26 A fool needs another one to state the object of regicide (13)
27 Dare change include return of an old measure? (9)

Down

2 If she has married him, Bob's your uncle (4)
3 Bored as soldiers on the parade ground (7)
4 The best tree for fuel? (7)
5 Recess for which authorisation has apparently not been granted (4)
6 Where bank tellers may be employed for the work of parliamentary tellers (8-5)
7 Obsession descriptive of life before starting work (13)
9 Stress in writing applicable to a tube service (9)
10 He doesn't volunteer to study the words of the act (9)
14 Condition in which late kings lay (5)
15 American lawyer turns liberal, quite off the cuff (2, 3)
19 Does she make some lad crazy? (7)
20 Strangle lout. That's odd! (7)
24 Many a quiet change perhaps (4)
25 It may be hunted in the forest again (4)

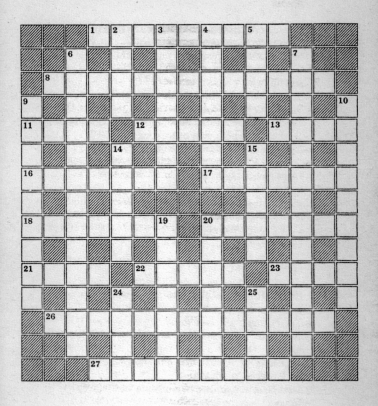

11

Across

6 Does he take the place of the lodger, when on leave? (10)
8 A far cry from the heart of London (4)
9 Meal so hot as to be almost untouchable (9)
11 Show anger with weeds? (4)
12 See 7 down
13 Crazy paths made for Keats's one-time home (9)
16 Architect on the wing (4)
17 Where an animal turns us round in Germany (7)
18 Cultivate one politician overwrought (7)
20 Disturbance three can make (4)
21 Doing as is required for identification (9)
23 Pole's length (3)
24 A pleased-to-see-you look (4)
25 Something generous to start the calling at bridge (4, 5)
29 & 30 Show dispassion as no usurer would (4, 2, 8)

Down

1 Carminative for a number suffering (4)
2 The atmosphere when Laura passes her test! (4)
3 Character from the Bible, a Hebrew one (4)
4 Layer round a piece of wood; it's elementary (7)
5 They're none other than little folk, speaking ungrammatically (10)
7 & 12 ac. One who is not even at home, apparently (3, 3, 3, 3)
8 Responses that are proverbially placatory (4, 5)
10 Spinner – none better? (3)
13 Upset at not getting a picking, maybe (7, 3)
14 Low breed revealed by Army doctor not attached to a current unit (9)
15 Withdraw from a catastrophic situation at the stadium? (5, 4)
19 Arbiter upset and cheesed, maybe (7)
22 Aggregate of foreign coin (3)
26 Feeling unsuitably shown in church at Evensong (4)
27 Palestinian plot (4)
28 Scottish cup news from Russia is its business! (4)

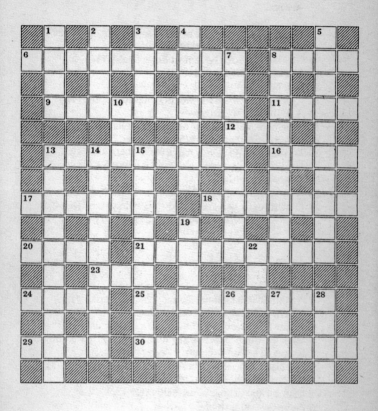

12

Across

1 Trouble between groups who won't share a racket? (4, 7)
9 Give ground of sound growth potential (4)
10 Patchy verdict on an accomplished actor (4, 2, 5)
11 Abandoned the British drive on (4)
14 Some information shortly to be read (7)
16 A couple of vehicles sandwiching a third (7)
17 A canvas holder (5)
18 Decline in status, but not much (4)
19 Unnoticed part of the ear (4)
20 Catches sight of about ten, though there are only two (5)
22 The introduction to a preamble was needed about here (7)
23 Not used in order to make transmissions (4, 3)
24 Work on the land or behind a counter, maybe (4)
28 Two masters, in a word (11)
29 Meat cut up for tea (4)
30 Message impulsively communicated (5, 6)

Down

2 A craftsman's calling (4)
3 Idols highly thought of in the theatre (4)
4 I enter a different course (7)
5 Suite of rooms that has lost its sparkle? (4)
6 Result of an appeal, maybe (7)
7 Qualifying condition for a Red Indian settlement (11)
8 Resolution that is forward in a large town (11)
12 Lyte words for solemn occasions (5, 4, 2)
13 Early days to retire? (2, 2, 3, 4)
15 Made-up accounts (5)
16 Men of the land no longer appeal to her (5)
20 Salvation Army lass once of great importance in the Holy Land (7)
21 They aren't good enough for export, but they help (7)
25 Rather like a grapefruit, it's more attractive than it sounds (4)
26 Quick way to get in touch if it's not the engaged signal? (4)
27 A short spin upsets her (4)

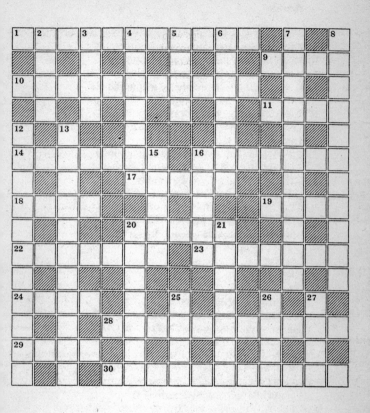

13

Across

7 When it does you see sparks, and bright insects (4-5)
8 Primitive weapon used for support (5)
10 The buyer of most cure prescription (8)
11 How one may be if a pin is twisted in (2, 4)
12 No longer is one divided by a hundred (4)
13 Rich land to be found in a veld or a dominion (2, 6)
16 Not well done, but that is unusual (4)
18 Urge a cockney male to take what the doctor takes (7)
20 Fat Poe said in a way (7)
22 Dissolute chap in the hands of a croupier (4)
24 I voted irregularly on a matter of loyalty (8)
26 Happy juvenile F.B.I. agent? (4)
29 'Full many a gem of — ray serene' (Gray's *Elegy*) (6)
30 Listen repeatedly for a sign of approval (4, 4)
31 One of a line for good measure (5)
32 Lack of experience which comes with spring (9)

Down

1 Devout circle in the name of popes (5)
2 Determined weight needed to support a big timer (4, 2)
3 Ship loaded with timber has no wake? (8)
4 Hesitation in one who attempts to dog (7)
5 Applaud rising actor's role which is nothing but empty words (4-4)
6 Nude's knit unravelled will be most cruel (9)
9 Look after a thoughtful entity (4)
14 Security breach caused by some drip or other (4)
15 Rash impulse put me wrongly into debts (9)
17 Air indicator used to start the plane (4)
19 Not disclosed (8)
21 Small university man is indeed made to look small (8)
23 They are weighed by craftsmen (7)
25 Letter from a patriot appropriately . . . (4)
27 . . . addressed as about at that time (6)
28 Wood which may be turned over to make a slab (5)

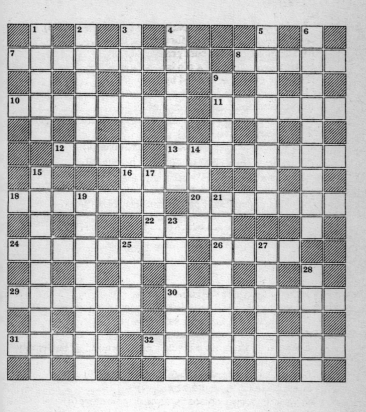

14

Across

1 Not so flippant a style? (6)
4 One expects from him an air of devotion (8)
9 Excited Negro going round a royal house (6)
10 Finds the pace too hot, yet is highly in favour of the idea? (6, 2)
12 A bit of music often changed (4)
13 Don't let him tempt you to do hackwork! (5)
14 Members of the French General Staff (4)
17 It shows what conditions may be expected (7, 5)
20 Chatty feature of a newspaper (6, 6)
23 A spindle or a cross is (4)
24 Festive fruit of dark appearance (5)
25 Does religious work (4)
28 Quite undaunted, I printed another form (8)
29 Advocates breaking into stolen Tasmanian capital (6)
30 Further writing on the other side? (8)
31 Incline to put off a decision (6)

Down

1 Goes down in a huddle? We're glad to hear it! (4, 4)
2 The remoter of two sides (4, 8)
3 A cutter on which one feels uneasy (4)
5 Not how one would define the role of Richard III? (8, 4)
6 Fishy sort of clue (4)
7 Gets charged with an offence and brought out (6)
8 Key worker taking pity somehow on a very good one (6)
11 It could be the sea rider's fondest wish (6, 6)
15 Exultant cry of a brave attacker? (5)
16 Meditate moodily upon one's little cares (5)
18 A series of local visits (3, 5)
19 A liqueur I declined before going outside (8)
21 A substance that will rapidly disintegrate (6)
22 A 16 down that shouldn't be left lying about (6)
26 One river rising in Nevada (4)
27 Ring up? So much for that! (4)

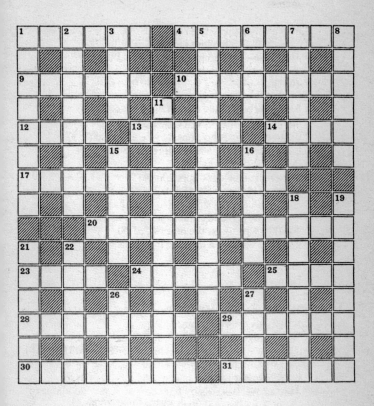

15

Across

5 Maybe the red traffic light gives a lead to the horse (6)
8 Simple chap, who hopes for a net profit (8)
9 Takes advantage of current dramatic productions, apparently (5, 2)
10 Stretch between two bends of the river (5)
11 Oriental always going around backwards at sea (9)
13 Farm workers make an attempt after ten (8)
14 Spoil the drink left on the paper (6)
17 One new age (3)
19 Philosophy which takes nothing from Zeno (3)
20 Some only short (3, 3)
23 Gambling game permitted in the course of a journey (8)
26 Amen puts an end to the argument (5, 4)
28 A brace of peacocks may (5)
29 Ruses if misapplied create a rift (7)
30 An attempt by Apollo that made Diana use her bow? (4-4)
31 Certainly where legal language is appropriate (6)

Down

1 Hard stuff is immaterial (6)
2 Strives for melodies (7)
3 Russian port for a godly servant (9)
4 The Tory Chancellor who was skilled at making cuts? (6)
5 He takes in young Alfred and Timothy when the referee blows his whistle (4-4)
6 The egg-producer stratum (5)
7 Oi! Secret organisation is meant to be secret (8)
12 Yes, the heart of 6 down (3)
15 Treating two articles singly somehow (9)
16 The place for a job (8)
18 Non-American archaism includes a number (3, 5)
21 Sin with a merry heart (3)
22 Precisely formal structure in the pig-pen (7)
24 Very often the favourite is the only boy in the family (4-2)
25 Private property of Oriental country (6)
27 Passage from a small island (5)

16

Across

1 Young sopranos who have reached a stage in their careers? (6-5)
8 The third form perhaps for a substantial body of taxpayers (6, 5)
11 If share prices rise he will certainly be grizzly (4)
12 Short passage to study out of context (4)
13 Wholly covered the legal argument finally (7)
15 Treason disturbs him (7)
16 Not happy about the French collation (5)
17 Make up for a flirtatious woman (4)
18 Insect upset by strong flavour (4)
19 Go in a bit; he won't budge (5)
21 What the courting bridge-player may do when he gets a better suit (4, 3)
22 Pa until arrangement of wedding (7)
23 It is received by letter (4)
26 Without doubt America backs Engineers (4)
27 What the happy whisky drinker keeps in (4, 7)
28 Compass declination when approaching rapidly? (7, 4)

Down

2 Its dramatic success may owe something to its bald picture of life! (4)
3 Puzzles which are full of holes (7)
4 Englishwoman and Frenchman who escaped the flood (4)
5 I shall, given employment, become badly treated (3-4)
6 In case the least is disheartened (4)
7 It sounds as though one should take a Conservative view – of the heavens? (11)
8 Turning out strikers means work for the marriage bureau (5-6)
9 Sent about ten letters of credit, very significant (11)
10 Public relations man? (5-6)
14 Derrick upsets 1914-18 volunteers with it (5)
15 In which to find young socialites a long time ago (5)
19 He puts up with a lot of constructive material (7)
20 Ted included a varied tour – by coach? (7)

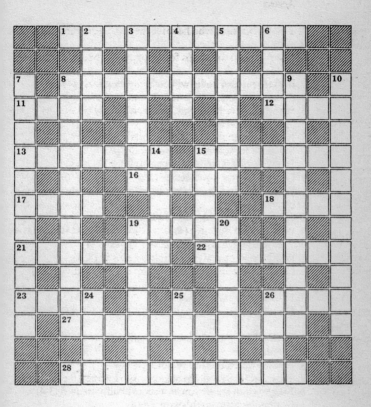

24 Book with an egocentric dedication (4)
25 To begin a circular letter a writer is needed (4)
26 Adds water, turns over, and there's food (4)

17

Across

8 Any combination of two notes (4)
9 A bit of food offered to a Norman cleric (3)
10 Three points about a tree of very poor quality . . . (6)
11 . . . set outside a stately home (6)
12 Talks nonsense about four serving men (8)
13 It generally shows where we are going (5, 2, 3, 5)
15 Glowing with fierce heat, and able to make an impression, apparently (7)
17 It naturally adds flavour to a dish (3-4)
20 Ingenious commercial practice? (5, 2, 3, 5)
23 What British Rail usually charge for a tot (4, 4)
25 Not quite good enough for a place of course (6)
26 It should satisfy those who hunger about what has happened (6)
27 The jumbo jet's fabulous predecessor? (3)
28 A water-carrier that has gone from the water (4)

Down

1 Boastful utterance wafted over burning sands (3, 3)
2 Didn't go putting a small pipe round a much bigger one (8)
3 The last command Houston might give to an impractical astronaut! (4, 4, 2, 5)
4 The nearest way to a stream of traffic? (7)
5 Try hard to put on a good show (6, 3, 6)
6 A regulation framed by men of intelligence for a Commonwealth country (6)
7 It can be a drag on progress when she holds the ring (4)
14 Inadvertently leave a trail, maybe (3)
16 A melody of vital importance (3)
18 The lady's revised clues had enormous strength! (8)
19 In essence, he requires cunning at the summit (2, 5)
21 Eastern garment at the back of the ship in a sealed container (6)
22 When small I ought to be giving Dorothy precedence over Edward (6)
24 He comes in for a lecture (4)

18

Across

1 & 5 O! A round robin? (8, 6)
9 Increase work for the summer (8)
10 Declaims like a whale (6)
12 Source of rumour in the hot-house (5-4)
13 Out of human chaos, a minor prophet (5)
14 Poet's black broken bone (4)
16 Top wool-worker, a revolutionary performer (7)
19 Such language from Suomi sounds like the end (7)
21 Stalk to stop the flow (4)
24 Wizard realm with an exhilarating air (5)
25 Otherwise ordering a South American flower (3, 6)
27 Old magistrates of severe disposition (6)
28 A tidy lot of charges for the stockman (4-4)
29 Praises quondam mixed lots (6)
30 Involved M. Rodney's concurrent symptoms (8)

Down

1 & 17 Petty cash, naturally, is needed for diversion at sea (6, 2, 6)
2 M.P. representative (6)
3 Open order? (5)
4 & 20 Instrumental compound of wind and strings (7, 4)
6 Formerly thoughtful, dear! (9)
7 Concerning pathetic borrowing (8)
8 Two girls in the garden of remembrance (8)
11 & 21 By-streets so classified as prizes (4, 5, 2)
15 Mrs Newly-wed fit for a house of correction (9)
17 See 1 down
18 Showing disrespect in R.Y.S. waters (8)
20 See 4 down
21 See 11 down
22 Heavenly messenger with a ring for a Shakespearian goldsmith (6)
23 One of the string told the French ceremonial officer (6)
26 Scolded at in debt (5)

19

Across

8 An actor holding the pit to be too masterful? (8)
9 New cord in from Scandinavia (6)
10 Get something down from the attic (3)
11 Predatory craftsmen (8)
12 He's holding nothing before us but the answer to the slum problem (6)
13 Be tickled to death, it seems! (3, 4, 8)
15 Tells how schools are organised (7)
18 After getting in the beer he went round preaching! (7)
21 They take steps to air their grievances (7, 8)
24 Arthurian knight about in a Philistine stronghold (6)
25 An Irishman who favours marriage? (8)
26 It's no good, I must have a couple of fifties (3)
27 Get back to do more shooting? (6)
28 Fixed ideas given a shaking and rejected (3, 5)

Down

1 Empty vessels I go after in a tin-mining area (6)
2 It's often child's play to put in order (6)
3 Impish thing to do (3, 4, 8)
4 A horse made of wood, perhaps (7)
5 Among the top 20 per cent preparing to take 'O' levels (2, 3, 5, 5)
6 Drinks to pass away the time on board, maybe (8)
7 Your actual team of stars (8)
14 Little fellow who is apt to 3 down (3)
16 Ran up half-yearly bills and supplies accounts (8)
17 They won a reform that is neither here nor there (2, 3, 3)
19 It secures no definite result (3)
20 Dynamic force that makes one act without thinking (7)
22 'I am myself indifferent — ' (*Hamlet*, Act 3) (6)
23 Warped desire to have a permanent abode (6)

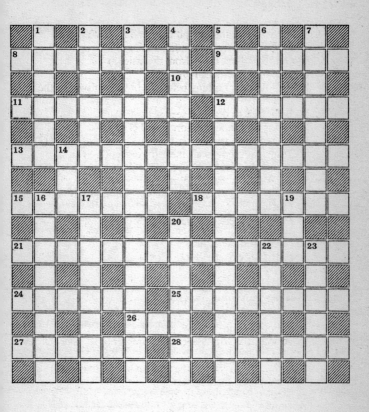

20

Across

7 Bureaucratic practice which a diet may be intended to prevent (7, 3, 5)
8 Spring back cover has been renewed it would seem (7)
10 Magistrate upset a porter (7)
11 Nearly headed off in good time (5)
12 Messenger of hope from a strange land (5)
14 A conquest repeated (5)
15 The merest trifle is imperative for action (4)
16 Go! The other way apparently (4)
17 Nothing is lacking from a court brief (4)
19 Backroom boy from North Africa (4)
21 Takes to the air as carriages of old (5)
22 Drain constructed for the very lowest point (5)
23 Fruit which comes in twos by the sound of it (5)
25 What the skeleton did when badly flustered? (7)
26 He rode for protection in the West, and used it (4-3)
27 Criminal traders' monetary resources lead to the worst of crimes (7, 8)

Down

1 Make a personal gift to perpetrate a revealing blunder (4, 7, 4)
2 Let, but not a single tenant paid the rent? (7)
3 Silly, silly Annie (5)
4 Account for the floor? (5)
5 Pretend to go about or be from strange lands (7)
6 People who are striking for considerable sums (8, 7)
9 Many a measure is quite stupid (4)
10 Plan to record reversal (4)
13 Much to which we object was, to the Greeks, food for idleness (5)
14 A cleric losing his head to crime (5)
17 A cretin, to be sure (7)
18 Bound and drawn (4)
19 Spoils of war (4)
20 Telling on the working terrier (7)
23 Breaking a plate is only part of the bloomer (5)

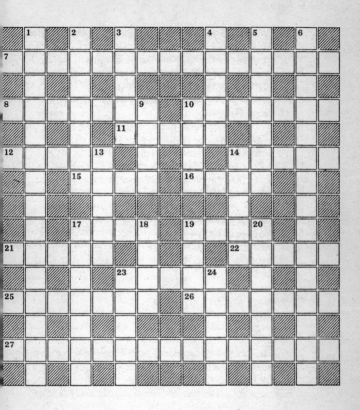

24 Move a batch of workers (5)

21

Across

1 Honest description of the company president's position (5, 5)
9 The poor offender may nevertheless think it a bit thick (4)
10 None the less – and none the more, either! (3, 3, 4)
11 The most proficient sailor in case (6)
12 Presumably a writer of drama in which babies are confined (4-3)
15 What the losing tennis player was to record? (3, 4)
16 Song which may be called in . . . (5)
17 . . . wrecked bus if there is a piano to start it (4)
18 East European leader to take it in (4)
19 Backed 500-1 favourite though not hot (5)
21 One from U.S.S.R. by the name of Smith (7)
22 Light unit to strike before Herbert is cut down (7)
24 Circle hills yielding fruit (6)
27 Scrub hypertrophy (10)
28 Black crushed bone (4)
29 Safe tourer designed to carry mum, dad, and the kids (4-6)

Down

2 The old battle-axe renders an account (4)
3 To vary R.V. may offend his religious commitment (6)
4 Cattleman producing more than is consumed in a pile (7)
5 He may have built it across the river Pison (4)
6 Feared being, in a way, both Red and dead! (7)
7 Get invoice all wrong and hand in your resignation (4, 6)
8 Leasing or releasing? (7, 3)
12 No change for the newsboy? (5, 5)
13 A physician to fool another about nothing but a diplomat (10)
14 Name all women? (5)
15 Pointed implement used by carpenter who is notoriously slow (5)
19 Imitate the departure of a plane (4, 3)
20 They may be awarded for injuries when mother gets older (7)
23 Moving abroad, visitor to India could visit it (6)

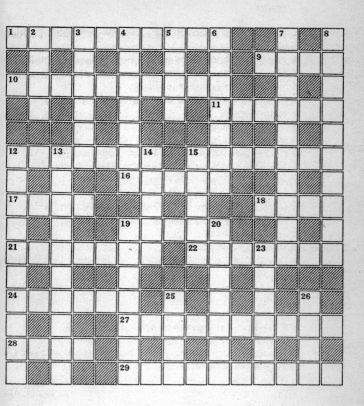

25 Furious driver who never saw any traffic lights (4)
26 The central feature of a nasty eye (4)

22

Across

6 The prudence with which the geographer may advance his interests? (7, 6)
8 Doesn't miss the ball, but cuts it very fine (6)
9 Plain constable about fifty-one blocking the way out (8)
10 One article is enough for him (3)
11 Grappling successfully with a top course in masonry (6)
12 A dunce that is disposed to give a formal interview (8)
14 A joke kept within bounds by my grandeur of style (7)
16 An old-timer unable to work in bad weather (3-4)
20 Clan assembled in a little bay for a solemn meeting (8)
23 Woebegone sergeant-major put face about! (6)
24 An export whisky from Canada (3)
25 A drop welcome to the consumer (5, 3)
26 Constructive fighters not in time to tell (6)
27 A petition that comes late in the day (7, 6)

Down

1 What the family doctor has leads to perfection (8)
2 Cyclopean feature of remarkable interest to the traveller (3, 5)
3 Old city posing new menace about X's follower (7)
4 Thwarted by someone seeded (6)
5 'Let none — That riches grow in hell' (Milton: *Paradise Lost*, Book I) (6)
6 Attended special lectures elsewhere and played golf? (4, 2, 1, 6)
7 A seaman hero of a story? (4, 9)
13 The traveller's joy, a well-known flower of the Tyrol (3)
15 The girl who is always in the middle (3)
17 Kind of service where an officer may carry his stick (8)
18 Norfolk town holding drama shows (8)
19 It makes one unfit to be in a high position (7)
21 According to this dog everything is as it should be (6)
22 Soldier's term for a piece of artillery that is put under a bridge (6)

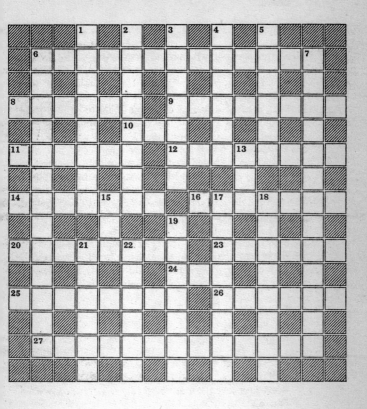

23

Across

1 Competitive flea-hunt in which no one is handicapped (7, 4)

9 Modern weapon which could be turned to use by fishermen (4)

10 Biblical reference can somehow be found in supersonic aircraft (11)

11 Ecclesiastical set-back from a note added to an afterthought (4)

14 Players may regroup for them (7)

16 Tennis game which tennis has literally (7)

17 Sense enjoyed only by people of vision (5)

18 A battery charge in which sappers desert the revolt (4)

19 Electricians' union has one small case (4)

20 Rise and dress (3, 2)

22 Ticket inspector for a sailing vessel (7)

23 No relation of the truthful short story teller (4, 3)

24 Not to remain a former French mandate (4)

28 Escaping fracture in an extreme disease (8, 3)

29 Ended on the other side, it would seem (4)

30 For this is precisely what global geography is about (3, 3, 5)

Down

2 Store in which poultry is kept (4)

3 A papist's description of current shorts (4)

4 Bottles for juvenile motorists? (7)

5 Dig out a lot of paper (4)

6 It provides shelter for the crew, the one that crew mine (7)

7 I put on tails, but make a condition (11)

8 Holes in which to bury before the street gets dangerously slippery (11)

12 Incitement to join a professional job (11)

13 Quasi-etymological examination of an entomological freak? (8-3)

15 King is overthrown by a hefty strike (5)

16 Silence is clearly excluded (5)

20 The soldier who is anything but particular (7)

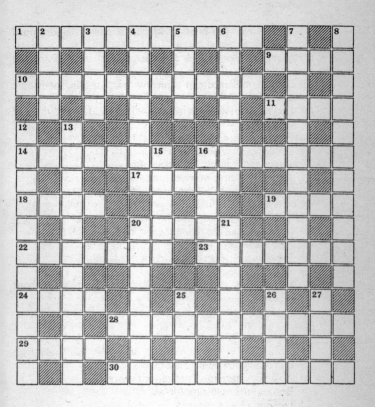

21 Hobby belonging to era between grandfather's age and
   ours (7)
25 It is added to a degree employed in angling (4)
26 The price of exchanging money from the bag I open (4)
27 John, a stock figure (4)

24

Across

1 One within still to be shaped in military habits? (9)
9 Member to ring with anger for a cupboard (7)
10 Peremptory demand for a rise! (5, 2)
11 A cut above a fillet (7)
12 Though far from relaxed, it holds everything back with comfort (3, 2, 4)
14 It saves taking flight to reveal confusion (8)
15 An order he's to stake out (6)
17 One who doesn't share our faith in the Athenian assembly (7)
20 Horror-struck at being rent by jagged gash (6)
23 The air of a tardy admirer? (8)
25 Adroit lie twisted to give an opinion of the press (9)
26 Temporarily sink two thousand in Eire's reconstruction (7)
27 I can't get involved with it on a very big scale (7)
28 Behave like a sluggard, though above falsehood (7)
29 Light fantasies? (3-6)

Down

2 An elevated narrative including one girl (7)
3 Devotee who urges his team to get on and flourish (7)
4 Form of gambling that is allowed *en route* (8)
5 Young woman who contributes to Amsterdam's elegance (6)
6 A goblin wandering, but not so bad (9)
7 I send a letter off in the Royal Exchange and get a quick answer (7)
8 Not a salient addition to the ranks of the sappers? (2-7)
13 Was hotly indignant with the germ about (7)
15 Evidently not a good rating, though that's what his superiors might give him! (3, 6)
16 Novel conception of heaven on earth (7-2)
18 It was exchanged in the finish for an unwelcome visitor in winter (4, 4)
19 A fast coach? What a lie! (7)
21 The animals shot hereabout may naturally provide sustenance (7)

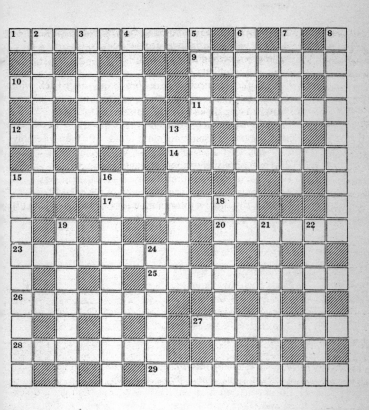

22 A play centre that can be made to admit us (7)
24 Considered taking action about the Middle East (6)

25

Across

1 Doling out punishment to a hefty youngster? (9, 3)
8 Relative with an attachment by no means salubrious (7)
9 No way to address a lady! (4, 3)
11 Inset it so none can be smaller (7)
12 Coat with uncomfortably hot spot in the pouch (7)
13 Substance to keep the Syrian capital in check (5)
14 Outstanding plan of Lucknow in 1858? (6, 3)
16 Foreshadowed the last of the wine, apparently (9)
19 Silent as one in diplomacy (5)
21 Payments that are a setback to a girl (7)
23 By-product of the petroleum plant? (4-3)
24 Beastly group of stars having one over the eight (7)
25 Amy who steals from the picture? Ask Dudley! (7)
26 Given it's money, it isn't enough (12)

Down

1 Minute parts not up to standard (7)
2 Dear one, how the school has changed! (7)
3 Got a flat in America (9)
4 Try on this river for work (5)
5 That pleased-to-see-you look (4-3)
6 Long hair was the death of him (7)
7 Intellectual gem? (7, 5)
10 Review a late picture suitably screened (12)
15 Acted as front-runner in the wrong way (3, 6)
17 Sprinted? You don't say! Where? (7)
18 Weave some points about a double (7)
19 Large number in high voice get a shake (7)
20 Calm worker keeping the flow of traffic going (7)
22 Pares back the rest (5)

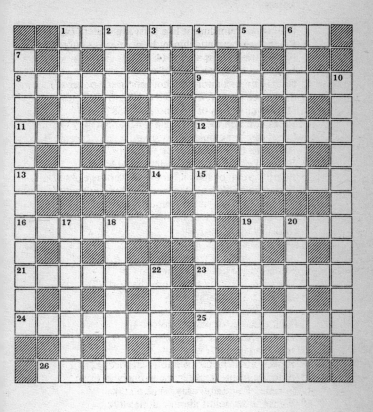

26

Across

1 The old mare's grey and not what she used to be! (7)
5 Baseball player who is a successful detective? (7)
9 Not for the first time a devout man is in opposition (7)
10 Vessel for the witless drinker? (4, 3)
11 Bed cover that is turned back and down after turning colour (5-4)
12 Crow-bar? (5)
13 Cord I twist into a sort of column (5)
15 Passed test as an opening batsman, it would seem (9)
17 Many I turned out and put on show (9)
19 What a luncher needs daily about one (5)
22 Material to fill up (5)
23 Enquiry relating to enquiry reveals the true position (5, 4)
25 Where letter-boxes are often put out of the weather (7)
26 An epitaph on the face of it (7)
27 Throttle great to adjust (7)
28 Evangelistic injunction to keep going, without the others? (4, 3)

Down

1 The cul-de-sac all mortals reach (4-3)
2 Wander, heading Middle East instead of West (7)
3 One taken in by Greek is beyond all aid (5)
4 Double-talk ditty about ring on cut timber (9)
5 Room on board taxi not out on a job (5)
6 To heretic a little revision is not practical (9)
7 In it the sailor spent the rest of his voyage (7)
8 Left off? Anything but! (5, 2)
14 Arctic battle zone pointed out on the map? (4, 5)
16 Try Cook's vessel (9)
17 Descriptive of a gallant in a hurry (7)
18 Lead-line in better condition (7)
20 Young Ronald overcome by pain current in the nether regions (7)
21 The only thing a defeated army can beat (7)
23 No need to do so, just make a stew hash (5)
24 Rescues five caught in rising seas (5)

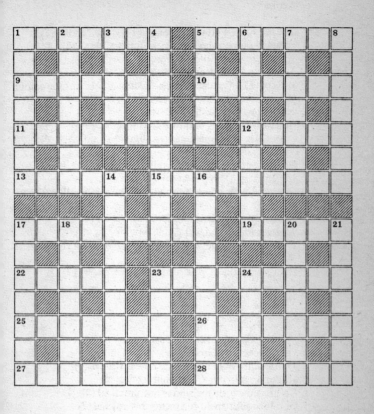

27

Across

1 Cutting short a vital operation on a space mission (7)
5 Females who are fairly representative of humanity (7)
9 Maritime power (7, 2, 3, 3)
10 A party or the means of access to one (4)
11 It naturally swims in a deeper channel (5)
12 Make a long journey by slow train in Africa (4)
15 Beset by wild herds it vacillates (7)
16 Double regard for an informal inspection (4-3)
17 Five airmen become the embodiment of classical wisdom (7)
19 Put in a request for a very quiet German song? (7)
21 The country is opposed to it (4)
22 American lawyer going round a cricket club in Bangladesh (5)
23 I go out after a special discount (4)
26 Spartans like Gabriel Oak and Michael Henchard (5, 10)
27 'Our little — have their day' (Tennyson: *In Memoriam*) (7)
28 Treats with contempt a relative by marriage? (7)

Down

1 Fish in fact put in the clear (7)
2 Verbal reassurances (10, 5)
3 The state from which Sir Andrew is derived (4)
4 Idly goes about to acquire handy devices (7)
5 Able to give both the short view and the long (7)
6 Hot duck rehashed for an emperor (4)
7 Report of a calamity quite the reverse of 2 down (11, 4)
8 He lacks the wherewithal to impose severe restrictions (7)
13 A precursor of bridge, perhaps (5)
14 A blooming suggestion of little reports! (5)
17 Strikers not allowed in a coal-mine (7)
18 The Indian tribe Pennsylvania feels hurt about (7)
19 Grants one form of current ties (7)
20 Makes a quick call to renounce vice? (5, 2)
24 Neat shelter not far from the Royal Exchange (4)
25 A plot made with care (4)

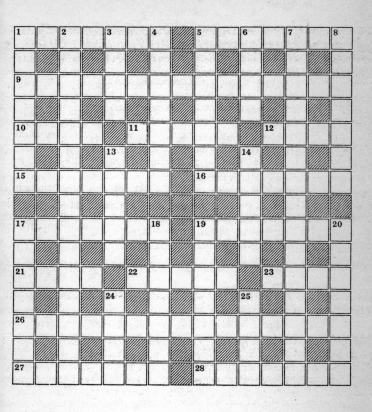

28

Across

1 Lady-in-waiting at the pastry-cook's (4, 2, 6)
8 Enrage a smoker (7)
9 Political fence-squatter started as a simpleton (7)
12 Conclusions shaped by divinity, wrote the Bard (4)
13 Heraldically striped maybe, in South Wales (5)
14 Back room for Othello (4)
17 A Member of Parliament in dire confusion was an adventurous mariner (7)
18 Singular extension for walking on cheese (7)
19 Heroic rover transported by Joyce to Dublin (7)
22 'For the — oft proclaims the man' (*Hamlet*, Act 1) (7)
24 Fancy counterpart (4)
25 Personnel support on musical lines (5)
26 Sell colloquially, putting game in retrospect (4)
29 Single Scotsman? Wise fellow! (7)
31 They hold up pieces and must be put inside (7)
32 He turned Bond crazily mad (5, 3, 4)

Down

1 Account the lady holds for surfacing (7)
2 First person on a Hebridean island (4)
3 Freely accessible setting in opera transcription (4, 3)
4 The funny bone? No (7)
5 Sang about horses (4)
6 Sign of a violent strike? (3)
7 Assorted doppel-gangers go to court gamely (5, 7)
10 Hostile craft in the main about to be reformed (1-4)
11 A bump on the head? He can explain it (12)
15 Prime tree, good fellow! (5)
16 Frosty old waitress! (5)
20 Rustic shoulder-piece on learner (5)
21 Glossy stuff can change seat round (7)
22 A loud moral story of good humour (7)
23 Recovered all in random ride (7)
27 Name transposed? So be it! (4)
28 Low joint where a cap is worn (4)
30 Three-quarters of an hour that concerns us (3)

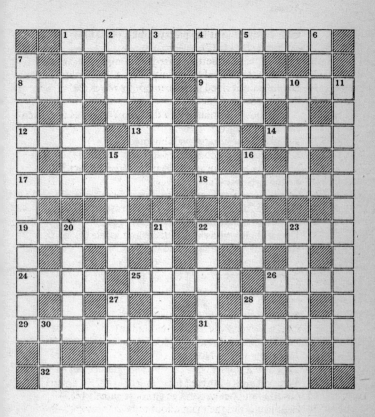

29

Across

1 A newcomer with a healthy complexion? (5, 4)
9 An article that will bear looking into (6)
10 Lean giant in need of being sorted out? Yes, assuredly! (2, 1, 6)
11 Crumpled hat found in a wood on the Kentish side of London (6)
12 Continued to 14 down? (7, 2)
13 Weighty theme of a song (6)
17 The river from which the skipper sailed (3)
19 A club ready to do evening work? (4, 3)
20 About ten really good reference-books ought to be! (7)
21 A measure to imitate on the stage (3)
23 Mabel and I resort to one of Maupassant's novels (3, 3)
27 Something to obey or dance about in (9)
28 It's not a permanent obstacle of course (6)
29 Sort of slave-girl on whom the rural economy depends (9)
30 'Alas, that Spring should — with the Rose!' (Fitzgerald: *Omar Khayyam*) (6)
31 He believes he's entitled to give a ruling (9)

Down

2 A property-man's income (6)
3 Work against society? (6)
4 Gave answers that were evasive and guarded (6)
5 Ring us about nothing? How unfeeling! (7)
6 An usherette pledged to voluntary service? (4, 5)
7 Established mode of thought (9)
8 A walk that can make one damper (9)
14 Not the proper way to 21 across (9)
15 New local cartel making a rough appropriation (9)
16 Class register in which there's a Pharisee, possibly (9)
17 Greek character from the tax office (3)
18 The wherewithal for making a small wooden tub (3)
22 French craftsman who made a special study of St Lawrence (7)
24 A note I'll lay odds about (6)
25 Outer space to the writer? (6)

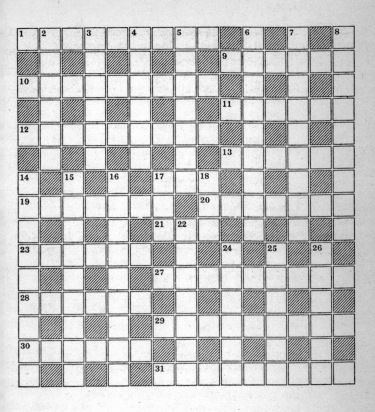

26 Scanty produce of a hundred scattered acres (6)

30

Across

1 The once-and-for-all method of railroading (9, 3)
8 Excluded nothing in the necessary equipment (3, 2, 2)
9 Diving birds who make a dash (7)
11 Persists in giving indulgent advice to father of lazy young man (5, 2)
12 Professional record, even though just someone's sideline (7)
13 Famous Wilsonian response to Common Market terms! (5)
14 Even a trip in the dark? (9)
16 First-class return following Middle East routes to Pacific islands (9)
19 Old Phoenician town is upsetting the fellow (5)
21 Familiar doctor gets a sovereign for amputating (7)
23 Lots of politicians provide entertainments (7)
24 Bounty, a big vessel (7)
25 Old-timer set on a pedestal (3-4)
26 Closely related girls with star roles (5, 7)

Down

1 One likely to draw in a difficult breath (7)
2 Middleman accustomed to being turned down (7)
3 A not unusual emergency telephone number for Roman emperors (9)
4 Finish on one's nose it would seem (3, 2)
5 Get up! Get-up! (4, 3)
6 Heath follows a Frenchman to the New World (7)
7 Employed poser to show how something operates (7, 5)
10 Feel toneless, yet contrive to get ready for a shock (5, 7)
15 Between them are scores of football pool entries (4-5)
17 Fodder in Switzerland (7)
18 Simplicity I've included in neat arrangement (7)
19 Unknown way over the hills (7)
20 They supply five hundred and one in butter (7)
22 Occasional winds in August sometimes (5)

30

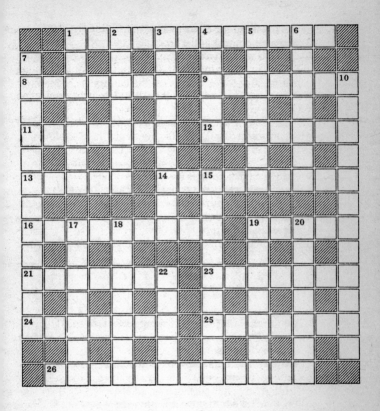

65

31

Across

1 Elite girl soprano? (5, 5)
6 Soup-making work (4)
9 My verdict after auditioning an acceptable comic turn? (7, 3)
10 Cannon blast which may strike the unwary yachtsman (4)
13 Well off, and not very friendly either (7)
15 A copper confronting chaps shows intelligence (6)
16 One amid a racket utterly fagged (4, 2)
17 Get up with complete rationality to act the disciplinarian (5, 2, 8)
18 Scene I compose for my brother's daughters (6)
20 Refer to all due changes (6)
21 Ties the rest scattered about (7)
22 What the man with a bell calls, certainly after a ring (4)
25 Grate for a pyromaniac (4-6)
26 Drawers of ships (4)
27 Maybe home-distilled liquor which certainly takes some beating (10)

Down

1 Two thirds of the feudal estate not subject to feudal tenure (4)
2 Tobacco advertisement (4)
3 Fruit with which a recognised painter is at home (6)
4 Appropriate but inadequate penalty for a glaring offence (5, 10)
5 Very little time to support the proposal (6)
7 Name the correct veto which United Nations supports (6, 4)
8 Person I met wandering by the Sea of Galilee? (5, 5)
11 The result of over-indulgence at the graduation parade? (7, 3)
12 Dog eats scrambled food – good only in parts (7, 3)
13 Lifeless coterie makes a determined onslaught (4-3)
14 Poles entering works can get sore if inflamed (7)
19 Points to a river which is very old (6)
20 A row of columns are enclosing the bounder (6)

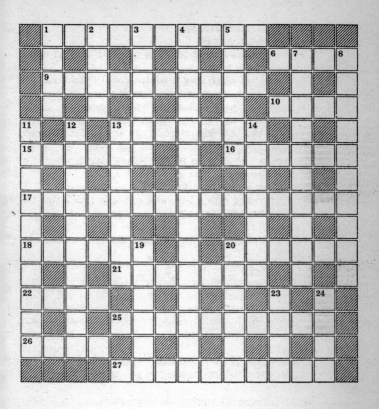

23 Anyone who employs you and me with hesitation (4)
24 Lily's a tot from 27 across (4)

32

Across

1 Sound resonant and harsh (8)
5 Conditions across the Atlantic (6)
9 In a similar way, a false statement about Kew is (8)
10 A herb that can be made to vary so (6)
11 Literally concerned with outer space (8)
12 Swiss home from which a letter may be forwarded (6)
14 Its constructors must meet very high costs (10)
18 Father takes her in when there's danger about on the border (10)
22 It turns more than once to an old master (6)
23 Move around to secure a sailor's dismissal? (3, 5)
24 Listener, thy end is lacking in spirit! (6)
25 Be fulsome in the face of a fat price increase (6, 2)
26 A Press organisation thinly scattered (6)
27 Implacable adversaries refuse to see this (3, 2, 3)

Down

1 Suitable monument for a regular feature writer? (6)
2 Request fresh air for an African militant (6)
3 A witty fellow brought up at home, the embodiment of perfect chivalry (6)
4 A drudge put into a French toboggan and taken out of bounds (10)
6 Young trainers coming from the races (8)
7 Fish stuffed with a little bread for a Victorian man of letters (8)
8 Tricky lawyers from 5 across who may have a go at Aunt Sally! (8)
13 Property-tax that presumably keeps the gamekeeper busy (6, 4)
15 Gives a sprinkling of comic talk on board (8)
16 A report I distributed in the Transvaal (8)
17 15 down girls at the foot of soaring peaks abroad (8)
19 A good man in the mine, though now too old for the job (4, 2)
20 A dish laid on for students? (6)
21 Main way to fasten sheets together (6)

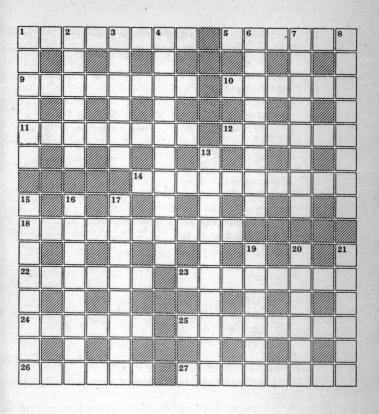

33

Across

1 Away, prima donna, and get some clothes on! (6)
4 Scholar with a fresh outlook (3, 5)
9 Gloss over (6)
10 Set upon, the stupid fellow went sick (8)
12 Time to reflect? (4)
13 Doesn't go with nautical guys (5)
14 Extent of first motorway annexed by the French (4)
17 In which enough gold is made on board? (7-5)
20 Could it be induced by spirits in large measure? (6, 6)
23 Five hundred years old! (4)
24 From the cost I assume it's port (5)
25 Net outcome of disentangling hems (4)
28 Bird giving one a shock after dark (8)
29 Woolly article to go with the Gunners (6)
30 They determined that fees should be altered (3, 5)
31 Official as Mr Bumble was (6)

Down

1 Winger with a lot to learn? (8)
2 Suit of carbon (8)
3 The prospect of an opinion (4)
5 Captain Jackson and The Old Margate Hoy, for example. (6, 2, 4)
6 Diversion unfolding 11 (4)
7 From which the priest advises how to mash potato (6)
8 Did some spooning in a big way (6)
11 How the theatre evolved, presumably (5, 2, 5)
15 Guide a sanctimonious bunch (5)
16 Snake, I see, sound, but all of a jelly (5)
18 Turning off the main way (4-4)
19 Rudimentary action in which he is involved (8)
21 Man of title has nothing to lose at this place of battle (6)
22 Hound a bird protected by British capital (6)
26 Mountain before ascending, and . . . (4)
27 . . . coming down to find a stake (4)

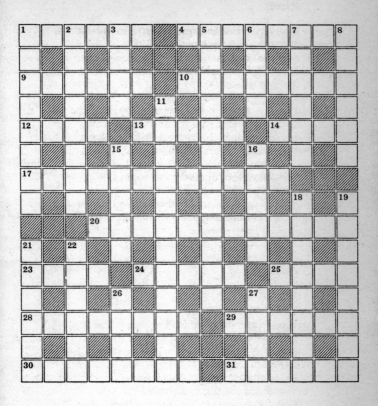

34

Across

1 They never tire of saying what telephone kiosks are to their kind! (12)
8 He wasn't born to rule (7)
9 A hunter disposed to bring something to light (7)
11 One youngster was bold enough to sling him out! (7)
12 It records only the shining hours (3-4)
13 Animals used for transporting copper coins from the Roman mint (5)
14 Ancient grudges dug up from Wisden? (3, 6)
16 'Only necessary to mention — and it appeared' (Dickens: *Little Dorrit*) (9)
19 He offers a piece of moral philosophy (5)
21 Assign work to a writer (7)
23 Haphazardly learns about a reserve of strength (7)
24 Rodent exterminators who seek and get medical treatment? (7)
25 He paid dearly for his brief vision of immortality! (7)
26 Angry rejoinder over the Bunsen burner? (6, 6)

Down

1 Partners who dance up in close formation (7)
2 Makes an entry, a footnote about fruit (7)
3 Light ditty dealing with unrequited passion? (5-4)
4 They resort to debauchery and rouse agitation (5)
5 Sort of cocaine coming from the sea (7)
6 Prior belted one that is ultimately right (7)
7 Off it goes as soon as the housebreakers arrive! (7, 5)
10 What the angler does while waiting for a number? (5, 3, 4)
15 Disjointed tirade about a health resort of quite different character (9)
17 Painting of an old Border raider going over a Yorkshire river? (7)
18 Bardic wear (7)
19 Italian food Rex is to turn to (7)
20 Mild combination of net and line (7)
22 Given relief from a disease difficult to cure (5)

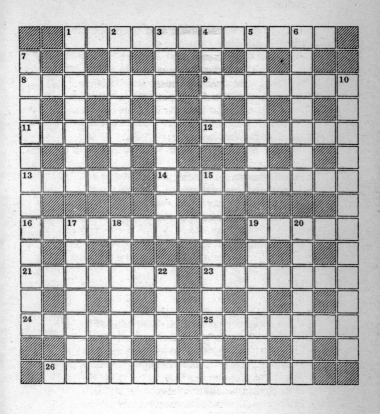

35

Across

1 To some degree, be a child (4)
3 In the oak forest it is painful on foot (5)
6 Point to a vehicle showing the mark of an accident (4)
11 A warning from the highest man in the Navy (4, 3)
12 A cheer for the falsehood of the highlands (7)
13 Brief description of a gin and It (5, 3, 5)
16 Holds up, as the policeman does (7)
17 Maybe the other shareholder leads him a dance (7)
18 Show taxi revised rate (7)
21 For non-Anglicans it was a set-back requiring diplomacy (4, 3)
23 Feelings about the future gift I'm somehow sent (13)
26 Worked in a house damaged by fire (7)
27 Hide one area of a Mediterranean island (7)
28 Account for Japanese liquor (4)
29 Beginning to break stone (5)
30 Not first hand employed (4)

Down

1 Certainly not a square dance (4)
2 Can't possibly be the only child in a monastery (7)
4 A blade would, only if he wished to insult the girl (7)
5 Gather what the ringside bell means (5, 2)
7 Offence ending with an allied campaign against Russia (7)
8 They have piles and piles, but are down-trodden (4)
9 Holiday centre rightly put out terrorists (7, 6)
10 Nothing but a blooming oration (7, 6)
14 Striking contest? (5)
15 Contrive to trace box (5)
19 Jeer the publican's counterstock of bottles? (7)
20 Twiddled the knobs but added a frightful noise to the melody (5, 2)
21 Steer it, to make an Adriatic port (7)
22 Articles on writing church music (7)
24 Account saint's written up (4)
25 Not quick – on the draw, it would seem! (4)

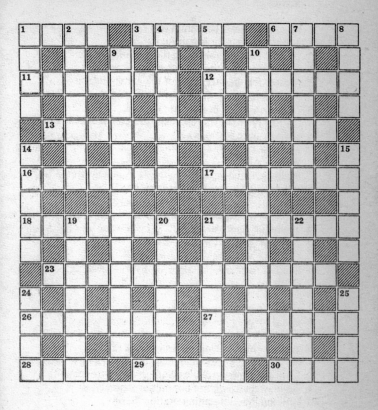

36

Across

1 Final act of wedding ceremony for joining together 'Him and 'Her' (13)
10 It stabs Pilot Officer beside a back ditch (7)
11 Exercise done by the criminal (7)
12 It flies on board (4)
13 Polite sort of servant (5)
14 Dismal Prussian maybe (4)
17 Getting ready to feather a circle of sailors? (7)
18 Wandering Scotsman returns with general assistant about one (7)
19 Survive everything except the final ball of the innings? (7)
22 His sales may be at cut-price here, but dear in France (7)
24 Part of the blind last broken (4)
25 Trouble-maker who starts any demonstration (5)
26 Underwater excursion to find an underworld retreat (4)
29 The fieldsman who hasn't been bowling for quite some time? (4-3)
30 Catch sight of smile G.P. gives (7)
31 Shady procedure practised by hybrid-breeding poulterers (5-8)

Down

2 The bitterness in what Franco urges (7)
3 No exclamation from him despite the torrential rain! (4)
4 United Nations acting to produce ruin (7)
5 Accountant Spain ordered to Russian waters (7)
6 Utopian dream? (4)
7 Annoyed with having caught about fifty (7)
8 The acid one could expect to find on a ghost-ship? (7, 2, 4)
9 Sort of bridge where apparently the trio got caught (5-8)
15 I'd back the vehicle to load it (5)
16 He strikes while the iron is hot (5)
20 A coach for horses, maybe (7)
21 Fractionally applicable to night of drama or day of grousing (7)
22 A nationalised industry should and did deliver the goods (7)
23 The sort of bend for holding full lock? (7)

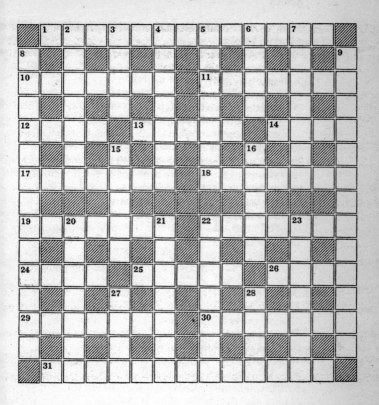

27 How to decide whether to take ship (4)
28 Accompanied by cleverness and humour initially (4)

37

Across

1 Time of year when there's less or more demand for pulverised fuel? (5, 6)
8 They show running totals on county 19 down (5-6)
11 A mischief-maker that gets knocked about on the ice (4)
12 Two points I'd included for the team (4)
13 A port in the West or East of France (7)
15 Was it danger that sent him to Arden or country love? (7)
16 Mawkish pages taking Chinese sauce round (5)
17 Tail-end of a noted work (4)
18 Plain answer to the accommodation problem, maybe (4)
19 Distraught girl clutching a sacred dish (5)
21 Makes sure an animal won't stray from the rest (7)
22 Small dwelling beside a lake for a limited number of people (7)
23 He preferred to deal exclusively with the Welsh! (4)
26 A fabric to fortify with spirit (4)
27 They are simply regarded as chips (6, 5)
28 Capricious desire to overtake? (7, 4)

Down

2 Taste of defeat? (4)
3 They are made to carry a great deal of weight in vehicles (7)
4 Bridging loans for diving operations? (4)
5 Conservative admission of love (7)
6 Scraps that offer chances of victory (4)
7 Formal request for something to put on (11)
8 Far too apprehensive to unbend? (6, 5)
9 Rich confection baked specially for Lambert, perhaps (6-5)
10 The dons seem upset by this fine old speaker (11)
14 Holiday suggestions put right in to us (5)
15 An eye for short measure (5)
19 On them we may base complaints when dogs run wild (7)
20 His temples are not of the kind raised to literary giants (7)
24 A dry turn for which a good voice is needed (4)
25 Rough-hewn temporal question (4)
26 The tribe in which Daniel evinced interest (4)

37

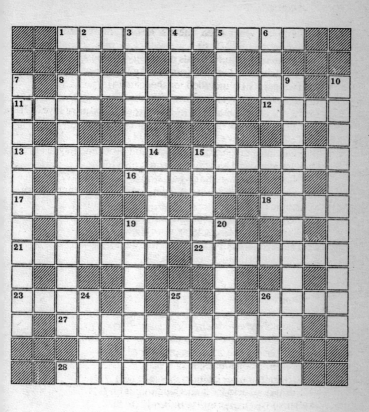

79

38

Across

1 The sappers not here? (5)
4 Swiss pass round French and make a fool of a fellow (9)
8 Heath confesses identity across the Atlantic (7)
9 In the process of taking over? (7)
10 Horses – or harriers! (4)
11 Coins once enough for underground fares (5)
12 They are sometimes used as missiles, in shells (4)
15 Lent dangerous mixture to one who looks down in the mouth (6, 7)
17 Guy Mannering's little dog (6, 7)
20 Sympathetic benevolent sort (4)
21 Back in honour, the inconsolable mother (5)
22 Latter part of frontier row (4)
25 Copy Australian non-flyer after due time (7)
26 The price of beer – it's growing! (7)
27 Befuddled, chooses R.N. vessels for drinking (9)
28 Tuck in Robin's band (5)

Down

1 Citizen soldiers playing on the railway? (9)
2 Combined under direction issued (7)
3 Put out when time's up (4)
4 Strides aboard as a sailor's right (9, 4)
5 Semi-resolute music maker (4)
6 Ringlet in disarray holds up the curtain (7)
7 Wine and water rules in Ethiopia (5)
9 Stock Exchange brutes (5, 3, 5)
13 Smith's striking support (5)
14 Ponder Dame Partlet's family (5)
16 True Roman turned fractionally above the line (in a vulgar way) (9)
18 Lucerne unrivalled (7)
19 Stumble on oil dispersed in Africa (7)
20 Maintains strongholds (5)
23 Light headwear all to the good (4)
24 Quiet little spirit makes money (4)

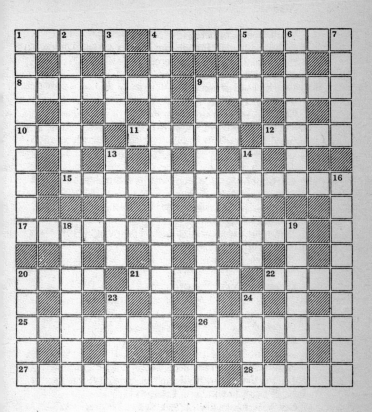

39

Across

1 Contrive and develop a fine way to shade maps (5)
4 Grand wine assortment travelling by a roundabout route (9)
9 Suitable game for rabbits! (7)
11 Chinese guild going round a Swiss canton on a sightseeing trip (7)
12 Characteristic smell of seaweed? (4)
13 A quaintly pleasing sort of accent (5)
14 Agonised cry of one engulfed in retrospective legislation (4)
17 Concession to the serving man with which Tommy goes home? (6, 2, 5)
19 Falsehood society is prepared to accept but doesn't often get nowadays! (6, 7)
21 I am brought in to take over, but worry (4)
22 Guiding lines (5)
23 Two cardinals about to do some packing (4)
26 Not a man put off by rice pudding! (7)
27 'Then let thy love be — than thyself' (*Twelfth Night*, Act 2) (7)
28 Highly developed urban communities (4, 5)
29 They run where he's the home linesman (5)

Down

1 Serious complaint modifying a ship that is T.T., and ... (9)
2 ... one that met with disaster of enormous significance (7)
3 Its object is to eliminate passion (4)
5 Sort of toll Aunt Fanny regarded as very serious (3, 2, 3, 5)
6 The world's second largest egg producers (4)
7 New item the BBC's old rival is brought in to copy (7)
8 Russian writer with two turns left (5)
10 A lot depends on it, of course (4, 2, 3, 4)
15 A small political group to note in Lower Saxony (5)
16 A time when blows are naturally expected (5)
18 Dissipated swordsman crawling over a beach (4-5)
19 A bucket of mixed fun that proves 5 down (7)
20 An undiminished number? (7)
21 Soup or hot stew introduced by British Rail (5)

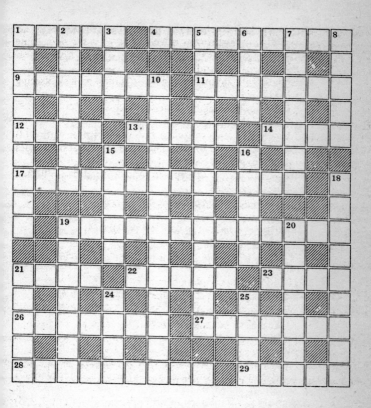

24 A tax put up to the Civil Service (4)
25 Pull in a bit when out for a ride? (4)

40

Across

1 The steam-engine era which gave electrical power? (7)
5 Bid one visit (4)
9 Do they serve in the ranks of a personal army? (7, 8)
10 Soak the head last if you want sturdy trees (4)
11 A lot of serving men turn professional in the Civil Service (5)
12 Painful swelling making you seethe (4)
15 Having an inclination towards playing nurse (7)
16 Lived in house rebuilt except for the roof (7)
17 Arrive by car only to find the approach under repair? (5, 2)
19 Coach for Guevara to tear around (7)
21 When the confirmed addict will need another shot in the same vein (2, 2)
22 Well dressed, like Alick (5)
23 It may scatter tugs (4)
26 Fine as the Antwerp ale well brewed (8, 7)
27 Is his bravery nothing to a woman? (4)
28 It always is following men turning one way and another (7)

Down

1 Make a clean sweep of the enemy (4, 3)
2 Still undecided, though believing the matter closed (8, 2, 4)
3 Not fully shut, it may attract wasps (4)
4 Note longer version of unbroken 21 across (3, 4)
5 Commonly a helicopter which docks? (7)
6 Your wife, Sir (4)
7 Hurried being a good deal behind? (7)
8 Instant reactions? No! (6, 8)
13 Records used by escapists going through bar by bar (5)
14 Racial classification as a Scot? (5)
17 The housewife usually has a brush with it (4-3)
18 It makes Tom pine for all-spice (7)
19 Duck from a fieldsman's return (5-2)
20 Answers produced by laboratory equipment (7)
24 Sees strange being (4)
25 Agricultural property for well-off Frenchman (4)

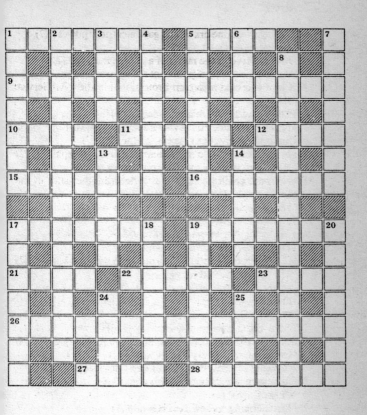

41

Across

1 Giving one's views on river defence? (7, 5)
8 The hangman's knot of silk, maybe (7)
9 Mark, what the book might say if it could speak (7)
11 A sort of name, one with a reason for turning pale (7)
12 Point to a cleric who builds up (7)
13 Dull doctor has only one listener (5)
14 Theatrical censor's ruling means curtains for the actor (4-5)
16 In the midst of evil, current home help is sweet indeed (9)
19 Support for the workers (5)
21 N by the sound of it to increase in size (7)
23 Refuse warm wine before a number enter approval (7)
24 Journey permit for only one of 10 down (7)
25 Little Annie very eager to get some cloth (7)
26 Using the linen mangle for mummy's dress? (7-5)

Down

1 The acre converted to metric (7)
2 English bishop the French watch (7)
3 One from the North Atlantic who is said to admit to libel (9)
4 Dirty result of extremely serious point (5)
5 Callously overload work on newspapers generally (7)
6 Order only painfully grasped (7)
7 Glowing pride of the pure-blooded Peruvian prince? (12)
10 All the same, it is a fairly good hand for the poker-player (5, 2, 1, 4)
15 Ten Romans designed artistic additions (9)
17 Murderous artist had a cell in one (7)
18 Old money thrown around cleared some obstacles (7)
19 The golden hush (7)
20 Not deigning to stoop to anything? (5, 2)
22 Beaten, beheaded, and chewed (5)

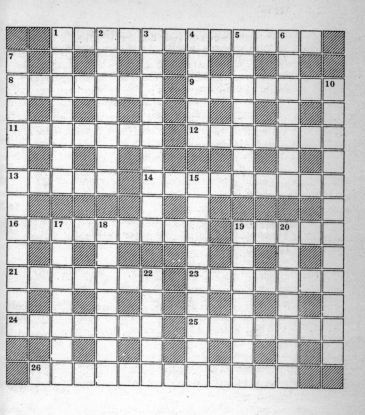

42

Across

1 Extreme view abandoned by James Hilton? (4, 7)
9 Liability incurred for cutting and pruning, maybe (4)
10 Mystic realm put into harmonious shape (11)
11 Part of the educated mind (4)
14 Hot core produces smoke (7)
16 Garbled report about a magisterial Roman figure (7)
17 Two small rivers intersecting vital part of Ireland (5)
18 A Hapsburg with no throne to return to (4)
19 In this case the points should be safe (4)
20 A news broadcast for the children of Scotland (5)
22 A handbill that appears in spring, naturally (7)
23 Famous Venetian who used to paint or draw game (7)
24 Sea-bird returning for others (4)
28 They ring for service (6, 5)
29 Labour party joke about nitrogen (4)
30 Hasty old man disguised as a poet (5, 6)

Down

2 Beef supplier going round New York for a cameo, perhaps (4)
3 Midland flower that certainly isn't wild (4)
4 Prospect denied to the occupant of an underground cell (7)
5 Mark II bird? (4)
6 Where one might pray for the talent of a Demosthenes (7)
7 It should be capable of dealing with a blaze, if I start one somehow (4, 7)
8 An aeronaut, who doesn't have to pay for the current he uses (6, 5)
12 A sign of youthful learning (6, 5)
13 Transferred to the dispatch department or dismissed? (4, 7)
15 A doctrine that doesn't change when put up (5)
16 'I love a ballad in —' (*The Winter's Tale*, Act 4) (5)
20 Why I get strangely ponderous (7)
21 Dignified tile! (4-3)
25 Lower court (4)
26 Chief character in 14 across (4)
27 It springs on its host uninvited! (4)

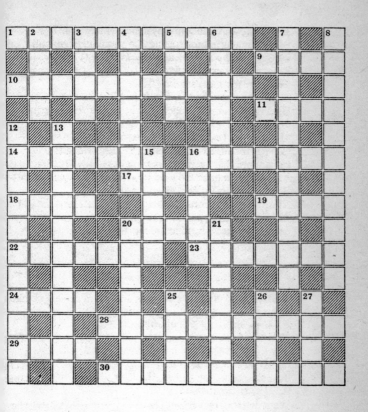

43

Across

6 The chances in favour of second-rate talents (13)
8 Bright cent, and something with which to get a purchase (6)
9 Left stakes about Navy light equipment (8)
10 What an Irishman would feel if his country were robbed of territory? (3)
11 Soft-headed noblemen wear them on coronets (6)
12 Underwear in the bottom of the drawer is a laughing matter (8)
14 Muttered, but not many at first spoke (7)
16 Enough to put Hebrews shortly in the grave? (3, 4)
20 He is more than ready to give a cue (8)
23 Assessing a seaman (6)
24 Eggs appeal to Virginia (3)
25 Apropos international problems U.N. must or disband (8)
26 Peer into the future, but do nothing (4, 2)
27 Empty gestures when famine hits (6-7)

Down

1 Talk with the other side (8)
2 Just a small island north of Scotland (4, 4)
3 Lays wagers about sick quarters (7)
4 Queen is overthrown, and may be burnt (6)
5 Mean man gets a note, but there is no trick to it (6)
6 Got better at cleaning the rifle? (6, 7)
7 Pi to the schoolboy, maybe (13)
13 Rival after five that is (3)
15 Grave letters worth a tear (3)
17 Bearings led Harry astray (8)
18 Rumps, yet timely sounds (8)
19 Demonstrate approval of 16 across? Hardly! (7)
21 Importance of short duration (6)
22 Set-up includes Ulster police for peace-time settlements (6)

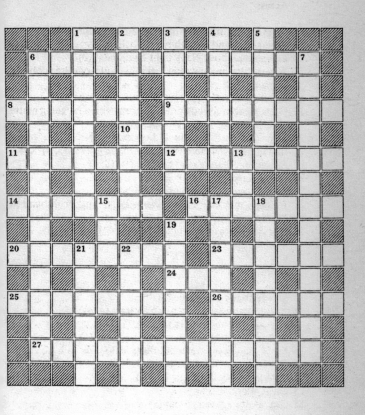

44

Across

1 Office of one who passes on scholarly information (9)
9 Malagasy tree-dweller always given an encore (3-3)
10 Gadget I can adjust when fruit is about (9)
11 A game that may put the ferryman out of business (6)
12 I ring back about the hour for a popular old musical (5, 4)
13 A burner burning (6)
17 Homeric character from the tale (3)
19 A mishap encountered while training (7, 8)
20 Coming out of the East, it flows South across Devon (3)
21 'I'll warrant she'll prove an — for the glass' (Sheridan: *The School for Scandal*, Act 3) (6)
25 Unsafe structure that hasn't any quick exit? (5-4)
26 A quiet name recalled for a very primitive type (3, 3)
27 Indoor game that doesn't merit serious consideration (9)
28 Mimic going round an overhanging shelter (6)
29 Harassed lady embracing poetry with disfavour (9)

Down

2 Status of the volunteer one up and dishevelled (6)
3 Texan who prospects for advice on creaking joints? (6)
4 Busy worker occupying reserved cabin (6)
5 Official claim for a share of the proceeds! (6, 3, 6)
6 It isn't slow to lift itself out of the water (9)
7 Callous and crusty? (4-5)
8 Oriental males in temporary dwellings shared by different families (9)
14 Fish on the Continent pursuing an independent line (4-5)
15 Old scoundrel unusually nice and smart (9)
16 The highest rises in all Europe (5, 4)
17 It sees a change of heart in 20 across (3)
18 Not a service of the slow sort, though it may count as one (3)
22 Potentially faster shell, maybe (6)
23 They like fish to turn and rest anew (6)
24 A river containing everything but a bit of frippery (6)

44

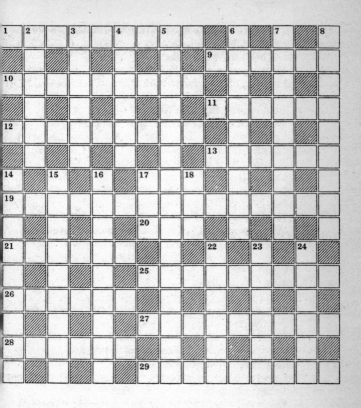

93

45

Across

1 Her turn finished, a brass-hat and politician go to the front, as understood (12)
8 See Mars in a royal guise (7)
9 Potted version of an old Japanese art (7)
11 Hopeless for a choice of letters (7)
12 Drama school subject (7)
13 Lulu hasn't half joined the sleuths, that's clear! (5)
14 An added strength for driving round the corner, presumably! (5-4)
16 Indicted at Balaclava? (2, 1, 6)
19 Bits for young jumpers down under (5)
21 Dog-carriage? (7)
23 Can a sea-bird have made Wordsworth so poetical about it? (7)
24 Come round again with a weaker concoction (7)
25 Wearer of the purple, though the tale has him in the buff! (7)
26 Net result of all efforts coming to nought (8, 4)

Down

1 Material make-up of two-thirds of a university over the century (7)
2 A process I'd added to the smashing of atoms (7)
3 Song of rebellion in a heated atmosphere? (6, 3)
4 Innumerable entertainers (5)
5 Canute's crazy, he is! (3-4)
6 O, the latitude of it! Hence its name (7)
7 One who, at a pinch, might have been an acquisition to Rugby (6, 6)
10 Landlady runs upsetting everyone (3, 3, 6)
15 It's given to some, achieved by others, Malvolio learnt (9)
17 Juicy offering of the same, in short, below Moore's 'Sweet Vale' (7)
18 Hang on to a couple of pounds, in a grab (4-3)
19 Geneva's fruitful source (7)
20 Overseer at the temple (7)
22 Concerning the first Mrs Ruff? (5)

Across

1 Two varieties of bacon, and game (10)
6 A striking suit? (4)
10 Drawing equipment for a sovereign (5)
11 The gem which should perhaps be planted on someone (4-5)
12 Cultural pursuits penalise skills (4, 4)
13 The main idea is the first singular object (5)
15 Dated book and French in content, dealing with intake (7)
17 Frightened by famous American gangster fully equipped (7)
19 A breathing-space (7)
21 Jumbo riders who, to some degree, shout wildly (7)
22 Sound from the cow carrying safe milk as a rule (5)
24 What Dartmoor farmers have to pay for heavy falls? (8)
27 A sophisticated crank in both a social and mechanical sense (9)
28 Apparently obtain promotion to board (3, 2)
29 Pole timber as window frame (4)
30 Tie veteran in knots as established (10)

Down

1 Commonly a girl the unpopular performer gets (4)
2 They measure everything included in adjusted prices (9)
3 Eat like a glutton, even though it is depressed area (5)
4 Mean the unqualified in great distress? (7)
5 Ocean commanded by Moses (4, 3)
7 Permission to go (5)
8 With less capital cover on verve? Rubbish! (10)
9 To discover money is no credit (4, 4)
14 Strange biblical book which cannot be wholly halved (3, 7)
16 Somehow bear iron aloft (8)
18 Raise the stake after 28 across, and it may blow its top (5, 4)
20 More recently an ecumenical treaty of 1929 (7)
21 It's a wonder a motoring club enters the mile (7)
23 Right marks for second markers (5)
25 High flier the beagle headed off (5)
26 No longer in the concert (4)

47

Across

1 Earthy means of attachment for a tortoise (8)
5 Quick respite in the Post Office (6)
9 An ecclesiastical point about a letter that's crossed another letter (8)
10 Prime object of care (6)
11 Rich seer involved in a jam, maybe (8)
12 A wine bar's small bill (6)
14 That attractive girl who has realised her high ambitions? (3, 7)
18 Still without a formal proposal (10)
22 Big wave that crushes whatever lies in its path (6)
23 One must be fit to have it (8)
24 Sailor in wretched surroundings, but having the capacity to survive (6)
25 One who has returned from the dead, yet has to storm out! (8)
26 Not at all like what might be tested (6)
27 Shallow impression about an old rebel of degenerate character (8)

Down

1 Cover that small church (6)
2 Artillery support for a fighting arm (6)
3 & 17 The highlights of an Arctic cruise, possibly (2, 3, 8)
4 Battling to keep the runs down? (2, 3, 5)
6 Show what one can do in practice (8)
7 Final courses taken up and emphasised (8)
8 In charge of players no means bright (8)
13 One of the men on board (5, 5)
15 The goblin didn't stay indoors, but got better (8)
16 Sturdy hole-borer held up in the beginning (8)
17 See 3 down
19 A place where moving scenes may be witnessed (6)
20 Bent tube filled with an inflammable gas (6)
21 How to prove one has a gong? Get away with you! (4, 2)

48

Across

1 Honest definition of an old-fashioned blonde (4, 3, 6)
10 Re-invigorate one new to force (7)
11 Refuse to go through verbal modifications (7)
12 One group in which 10 across may be found (4)
13 How the sailor is taken by a head-wind – surprised? (5)
14 Chain-work to protect the post (4)
17 Proverbially and policy-wise the best bloomer (7)
18 Mater in disorderly dress (7)
19 Fruity leading lady of the harem (7)
22 Bearing in arms a medicinal tablet (7)
24 Man-eater of Anglo-Greek extraction (4)
25 Liberals provide cover for skin-heads, one hears (5)
26 In the middle of advertisement about a note (4)
29 Involved with me, Lorna becomes a professional distributor (7)
30 Hide treatment centre for an old coin, and why, so to speak (7)
31 Captives mean to make fun for children (9, 4)

Down

2 Sell lots of game (7)
3 Unruly mob put to flight (4)
4 In a remarkable way, but not efficiently (7)
5 A shake-up for the motor-cyclist's passenger (7)
6 Strange Scottish gun-cotton ingredient (4)
7 Heritage, lacking aspiration, distributed in Surrey (7)
8 Designing female who might amuse herself on the board (13)
9 Festive occasions when the mail arrives from Moscow? (3, 6, 4)
15 A reprieved sacrifice is a small account nominally (5)
16 Canal purchaser, alias vertiginous Victorian (5)
20 Spurred on, he makes a bit in a livery way (7)
21 Disturbed reach on Virgil's woeful river (7)
22 Not so heavy a craft (7)
23 Figures in the O.T. (7)
27 Stops means tests? (4)

28 Sycophant worked at last (4)

49

Across

1 Suitable ending to a private war, perhaps (6, 6)
8 Too tense to knock something down? (7)
9 He's starred in Westerns (7)
11 The gods largely given a new look (7)
12 Small vegetable everyone has a guess about (7)
13 Three points I'd included as extras (5)
14 Accused of taking part in an attack? (2, 1, 6)
16 A cricket club medal I cast with public approval (9)
19 This law was designed to deal exclusively with women (5)
21 A footman who has to compete with others and worries? (7)
23 London lawyer capable of becoming M.P. later (7)
24 Big noise changing gear outside a Berkshire centre (7)
25 An atrocity dismissed with hot resentment (7)
26 Do-it-yourself home for distressed craftsmen? (6, 6)

Down

1 Deprived of natural protection and damaged by fire, maybe (7)
2 What the crow does when she comes in? Nuts! (7)
3 Document required for admittance to the beginners' class? (5, 4)
4 Trials in which only internationals participate (5)
5 Not the real reason why a see needs reorganising (3-4)
6 One who toys with something sweet, right? (7)
7 In such conditions no clear progress can be expected (5, 7)
10 It helps to create a feeling of comfort by giving complete cover (6, 6)
15 4 down held in a studio, possibly (9)
17 Ran wild in prison, causing widespread loss of life (7)
18 It colours things twice in ale correctly brewed (7)
19 Sum a skill up in the Malay Archipelago (7)
20 Early Protestant noble clutching a £2 return (7)
22 Something one is entitled to rectify (5)

50

Across

1 Maybe the only way to escape from a cul-de-sac is to resign (4, 3)
5 Nap enjoyed by the successful fortune hunter (4)
9 Presumably its subject is crime, and punishment (8, 2, 5)
10 Ship's officer to make a final check (4)
11 How most adverbs end. Twig? (5)
12 Blacken daily (4)
15 With all quantities minus, enough to bamboozle (7)
16 'Like a — in the sky' as Carroll said (3-4)
17 One who contemplates the work of Rodin (7)
19 Qualified as a bride in white? (7)
21 Metal used for making . . . (4)
22 . . . sort of plate (5)
23 Three points about a dying songster (4)
26 Appropriate wear under a shooting-jacket? (6-5, 4)
27 Run away and feel strange (4)
28 Perhaps the fourth taw, streaked and veined (7)

Down

1 He deserves to win, but doesn't get the girl (4, 3)
2 Faithful in work, the French provided a seat of imperial power (14)
3 A person's answer to 513239×21649 (4)
4 Recommended procedure when Tom is upset with twitches (7)
5 An onlooker not content to look on wickedness? (7)
6 It sounds like a burden on the prospector's mind (4)
7 Holder of burning and smoking waste (3-4)
8 Henry's first and last choice with a revolver certainly makes the sparks fly (9-5)
13 A barb which just happened to come off (5)
14 Non-Christian god inlaid with silver (5)
17 It puts an end to pricked fingers (7)
18 It may lead to a leper's retreatment (7)
19 Dash with a bovine bellow up to the café (3-4)
20 Indicated, but not in a legal document (7)
24 Inform William (4)

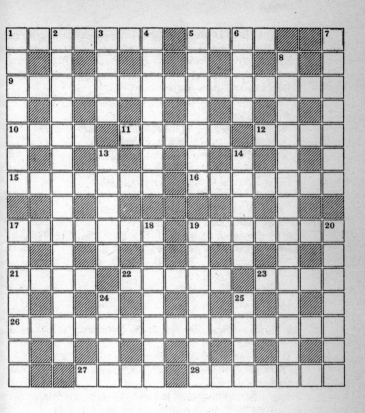

25 An arm raised overseas perhaps (4)

51

Across

1 Get under way now the stage is empty (4, 3)
5 Made an attempt to go around very softly, but missed footing (7)
9 Inaction or parts thereof! (15)
10 Don't leave Kate upset (4)
11 I cause injury returning to the American beach (5)
12 A bit of the alphabet ancients used (4)
15 A single transaction in the estate business (7)
16 Presumably it may lead to a marriage of religions (7)
17 A couple of hundred around Aden point to the rise and fall (7)
19 Given instruction in trade arrangement (7)
21 Painful outcome of electricity and high explosive (4)
22 Egyptian god claiming to be a Scotsman (5)
23 Misled, the doctor leaves for it (4)
26 Maybe cheques drawn on them are the goods! (8, 7)
27 Break up an underworld gang (7)
28 Animal concealed within cane structure (7)

Down

1 What 26 across may supply in the form of . . . (7)
2 . . . fine grit in foot-holds followed by fast runners (6, 3, 6)
3 Decapitated boars, sometimes feathered (4)
4 One way of reducing footballers who are over-smart (7)
5 Barber is tidier (7)
6 Anti-Ulster organisation linked with the North country (4)
7 Capital charge may lead to its being put (5, 2, 4, 4)
8 Toothy study given to an art gallery (7)
13 Naiad transfigured into goddess (5)
14 Insult that may be wiped out (5)
17 Many hurt by a witch perhaps (7)
18 Uppish Ted leaves determined to be like a lord (7)
19 Disturb new butler about nothing (7)
20 Maybe where liners each first get up speed (4, 3)
24 Articles of divinity (4)
25 Pinch the head off a little way (4)

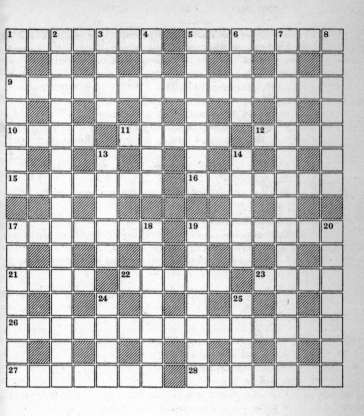

52

Across

1 Somewhat delirious device for penetrating the gloom? (9)
9 One way to eliminate a faulty service in a river (6)
10 They aren't fancied as competitors of course (9)
11 What liquid does when on fire, possibly (6)
12 13 across characters who add power to a circus performance (6, 3)
13 Sturdy old boy in reddish-brown coat (6)
17 An article not held centrally (3)
19 Its followers are bound to make an unfortunate impact (9, 6)
20 Not a bachelor knocking back a drop of refreshment! (3)
21 Brave talk? (6)
25 Work-shy Chinese secret societies that are remotely up-lifting (4-5)
26 One under a new order, though no stranger to it? (6)
27 Plain yet to be located, apparently (9)
28 'Tho' much is taken, much — ' (Tennyson: *Ulysses*) (6)
29 Good man to get through the batsman's defence and duck cruel punishment (9)

Down

2 Moral justice to which many players subscribe (6)
3 Bob stored for a tyrant (6)
4 I'd turn in first, then go for colour (6)
5 A lucky drawer? (9, 6)
6 In this way lions come to indicate a pause in writing (9)
7 What a draughtsman will use to compile a crossword, maybe (3, 6)
8 Its occupant stays put when retiring (3-6)
14 Reluctant to give credit (9)
15 Notes that must not be gone through quickly (4, 5)
16 Sort of body I'd see flouted (9)
17 Old war-god with the wit to turn up (3)
18 An object from which men derive inspiration (3)
22 After my work I have a complaint (6)
23 Burning rubbish dump on which it might be profitable to speculate (3, 3)

52

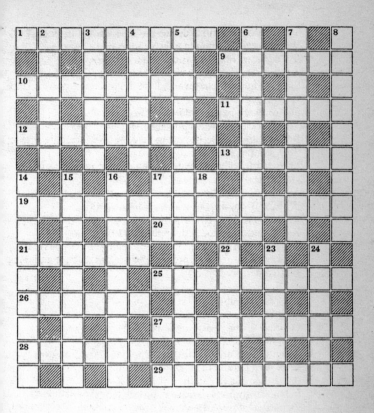

24 Elderly Engineers inwardly of one mind (6)

53

Across

1 Law and order men, not wives of desert tribesmen (8)
5 Wise man takes in one learner for food (6)
9 & 10 In a manner of speaking, what one expects to hear in the U.S. (8, 6)
12 Strike? One of a series (4, 5)
13 A course of the third degree; perhaps (5)
14 Stylish bird lacking understanding (4)
16 Simplicity of a net I've unravelled (7)
19 In good time one shouldn't be (3, 4)
21 Low point to observe listlessly (4)
24 Must X's follower be stale? (5)
25 How to scoop the pools, maybe (9)
27 Asinine variety of orange (6)
28 It's least common, possibly, in arithmetic (8)
29 Rock that's a degree ahead of the sailor (6)
30 How one dragon met its end, don't you know! (2, 6)

Down

1 Song of the hut (6)
2 Could be 7-0, notwithstanding (4, 2)
3 Dialect I'd bring back in the Isle of Man (5)
4 Wild about its rise in French currency (7)
6 The way Sir Percy Blakeney went about his revolutionary work (9)
7 Bitter though better halves of fish? (8)
8 No longer soundly mourned, but praised (8)
11 Language to quieten and curtail (4)
15 A repast one may leave composed after a breather (5, 4)
17 Strange discovery in a ruined Moab tomb (4, 4)
18 Discontinued line in cheap underwear yachtsmen secure? (8)
20 See the Scottish river in turbulence (4)
21 Hermes in his element (7)
22 Good shot of a pin-up in sappers' retreat (6)
23 Venerate a famous rider (6)
26 Port most worthy theologians take in (5)

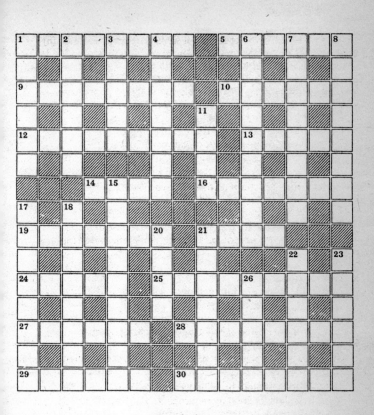

54

Across

6 Impressive collection of staffing economies in Fleet Street? (5-8)
8 Gives a different set of features (6)
9 Leave the country to celebrate? (2, 2, 4)
10 She means to seek legal redress (3)
11 Brings eating out to a fine art (6)
12 Doubly through being burnt? (8)
14 Ill-starred men of commerce (7)
16 Best blooming part of the year! (3-4)
20 Famous actor giving description of a bloody end! (8)
23 A chore specially prescribed for the Latin class, maybe (6)
24 Nothing left in retrospect (3)
25 Spin out a short professional treatise (8)
26 First-class fruit brought back for a character in *Othello* (6)
27 It doesn't exactly tell one what to expect (5, 8)

Down

1 Has he gone into debt in a new form? (8)
2 His opinion is sure to be of some value (8)
3 Old town requiring many centuries to grow (7)
4 Solid tribute to a distinguished citizen, perhaps (6)
5 A French diet oddly brought together (6)
6 An impression that should be corrected by the careful reader (8, 5)
7 Invention that has vastly speeded up the formation of habits (6-7)
13 A skate that goes through water (3)
15 Sin from which one never recovers (3)
17 Well fitted to be a competitor of course (8)
18 Extremely important part of a circuit (8)
19 It tends to confuse one who has to do oral examinations (7)
21 Prepare a scheme to evacuate? (3, 3)
22 A constable holding a male ruffian in Paris (6)

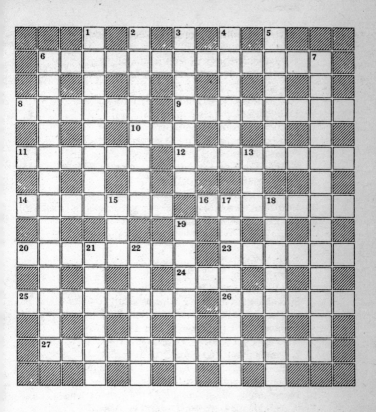

Across

1 Type of government which a foreigner takes to heart (5)
4 A matter of policy in U.N.'s race resolution (9)
9 Ten return lest somehow they raise blisters (7)
11 Limit appropriate punishment for a swindler maybe (7)
12 China set to New Guinea (4)
13 Is it possible for New York to be shrewd? (5)
14 Many an Ascot creation causes talk (4)
17 Be conscious one's not in the pink? (4, 3-6)
19 It may be true to life, but its characters never were (4, 2, 7)
21 Price of a ticket for the Far East (4)
22 It doesn't deserve white feathers, so remove them (5)
23 Courageous animals (4)
26 Get mine together for an assembly (7)
27 Smoking-jackets? (7)
28 Sacked when a large figure is not achieved (9)
29 Educated lad as a member of society (5)

Down

1 Puts on weight – that is what heated dripping does (4, 2, 3)
2 Earnest in adding a verbal condition (7)
3 Zero point in Egypt (4)
5 Is he responsible for keeping watch on board? (6, 7)
6 Call a gambling clique perhaps (4)
7 Therein change has a doubly exclusive result (7)
8 Leave out invitation to the hungry (5)
10 Where senior officers are taught to provide teachers? (5, 8)
15 French town advertised by travel agencies (5)
16 Coats designed for the opera (5)
18 Child carries a garment support for those who sponge (7-2)
19 Civilians who spot military hideouts? (7)
20 Wholly disorganised soldiers may be sustained here (2, 1, 4)
21 Well-known fancy about the Middle East (5)
24 Two conditions upset her (4)
25 The sort of steam-engine which today produces a smile (4)

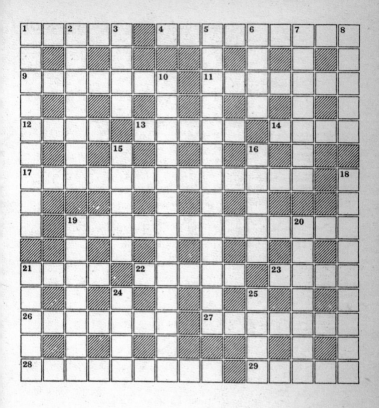

Across

1 Learner entered to try his hand against others, and finished (8)
5 Odds against a débâcle connected with Brussels (6)
9 Appropriate companion to the sandwich for a beach picnic? (4-4)
10 Apparently there is nothing now like umbrellas in the rain (4, 2)
11 The kind of passenger accommodation suitable for a single master (3-5)
12 Drink which lacks body (6)
14 The top 50 per cent mate (6, 4)
18 City to the North is the making of a writer (10)
22 Sea-bird with outsize victim for food (6)
23 In a religious sense he believes in coasting freely (8)
24 Given to stylish habits (6)
25 Morning of return to divorce centre with no retraction (8)
26 Timely job for a romantic antiquarian (6)
27 Cardinal feature of hilly country (8)

Down

1 Container for vehicle over 20 hundredweight (6)
2 Made fun of the sham press chief (6)
3 So call assembly for the villagers (6)
4 Gets courage, and trumps with a spade, diamond or club (5, 5)
6 To do so is an after-dinner practice that facilitates international proceedings (8)
7 Aging vision suggesting an unfulfilled ambition (3, 5)
8 The sheriff's officer who gives gratuitous advice to an employer (8)
13 Pious man takes young Ronald to a horse attendant – but not for breaking in! (6-4)
15 Electric current and equipped with flex; all as agreed (8)
16 The object of a marriage bureau – as to find her! (4-4)
17 Henry Jekyll's friend keeps talking apparently (8)
19 Up-to-date as the Navy after a fashion (6)
20 Old trust in opposing points scattered in days gone by (6)

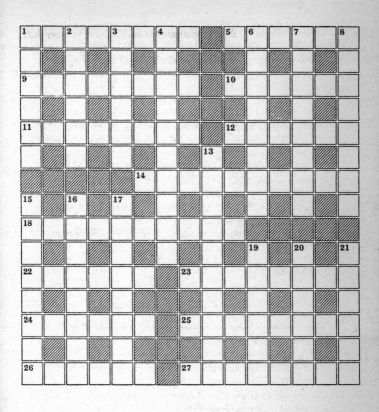

21 Candlestick for a crown (6)

57

Across

8 Speech from one's lord in the days of Viking rule? (3, 5)
9 Was the first man with a title, apparently (6)
10 Such a drowned valley is clearly the reverse of dry (3)
11 Do nothing for the time being with some mesmeric influence? (4, 4)
12 New nose-rings required for the round-up (6)
13 What one may do if one marries 20 down, alas! (6, 2, 7)
15 A recommendation for good conduct, maybe (7)
18 Russian fighter with the speed to fly from one country to another (7)
21 Holiday-makers find them highly attractive (8, 7)
24 Writing or broadcasting requirement (6)
25 Make out a document to be older than it is (8)
26 I reflect the way of an inanimate object (3)
27 Fragmented design of a memorable lawgiver (6)
28 Intemperate king in up-to-date environment (8)

Down

1 Left in a recess? Yes, a recess (6)
2 Not calmly collected at the frontier? (2, 4)
3 Maybe military training on which the independent doctor depends for a living (7, 8)
4 Extremely like a saw (7)
5 One can't go straight ahead and do this (6, 9)
6 A motorist who has swallowed nothing may have to drive him home! (8)
7 In the main it's regarded as a pest (5-3)
14 A chatterer that is after quiet (3)
16 Underground fare? (4-4)
17 Others must die if his way of life is to be preserved (8)
19 A miniature railway coming up on the Firth of Clyde (3)
20 With inconsiderate speed I go over the ruins of Athens (2, 5)
22 Make an investment in the church, possibly (6)
23 It doubled up an old master (6)

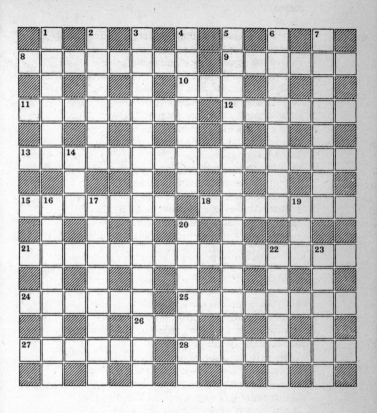

58

Across

1 Ran back scolding, telling the tale (9)
9 Old boy in gang is certainly game (6)
10 Skill expected of a right-hand man (9)
11 Treats indiscriminately for money in old Greece (6)
12 Cook's continental discovery concocted as a ritual (9)
13 Drilling is so monotonous! (6)
17 Encourage what beggars have in bars (3)
19 Where Castro's heart is faithless (7)
20 Visible perspicacity (7)
21 Baffin Bay's aid to swimmers (3)
23 After a little work, it turns on freedom of choice (6)
27 The unemployed for whom, said Dr Watts, there's diabolical mischief (4, 5)
28 To have fun on board, one way and another (6)
29 Paying what's previously unsettled (9)
30 Required of French in necessity (6)
31 Blooms from the seed Lewis scattered (9)

Down

2 Way to a rendezvous? (6)
3 Arrange crops wheel-shape (6)
4 Seaman Scot on the road (6)
5 Almost none is a close neighbour to it (7)
6 A starting point for those prepared for a row (4-5)
7 Noted as true love's gift in some branches (9)
8 For scrambled 17 across, a great assembly (9)
14 The car from Limoges (9)
15 Specification for those most easily suited (3, 3, 3)
16 Recommends lawyers (9)
17 The Spanish folio is brief but a spritely one (3)
18 It traps the spirit (3)
22 Cross indeed, to be ordered to provide references (7)
24 Happened our expeditionary force was given an inch? (6)
25 It's wicked, but make light of it (6)
26 A college fellow is Aphrodite's beau (6)

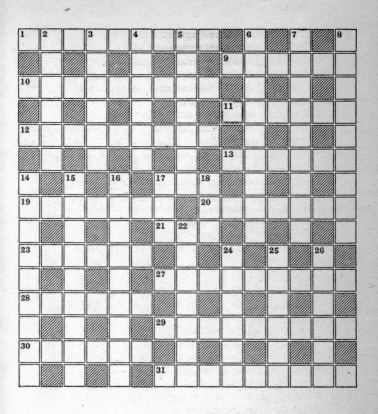

Across

1 A law passed to give everybody a fair share? (7, 3)
8 Able to help us with processed fuel (6)
9 Self-financed lowland pleasure jaunt . . . (5, 5)
10 . . . from which nothing clear may emerge (6)
11 Lines that convey heartfelt admiration (4-6)
12 Openings for craftsmen (6)
13 He won't turn out to cut (4)
15 One who obtains a concession from a regent (7)
19 Silver ring washed up on beach (7)
21 It isn't required to diagnose a superficial complaint (1-3)
22 Two bills I get with a tree (6)
25 Actors are prepared to appear in it (4-2, 4)
27 Put a fresh face on an agent about five in the morning (6)
28 A working reserve (6, 4)
29 Small sweetmeat of agreed constitution (6)
30 The rest of creation? (7, 3)

Down

1 Hitting the ball with the meat of the bat, though not particularly well (8)
2 Lively turn I've put on (6)
3 Difficult poem by Christina Rossetti (2-4)
4 A bird, for example, put in a bath to soak (5)
5 Earning an honest penny as an informer, maybe (8)
6 Tattered glories investing a secluded part of the Ottoman court (8)
7 Conditional statement? (8)
13 A lady's man, right? (3)
14 Progress, for instance, and how! (3)
16 Science that has taken man out of his sphere (8)
17 Only notes required on a through journey? (2, 6)
18 They illustrate what happens when Max turns over in troubled sleep (8)
20 Slim lady arrayed in depressing fashion (8)
23 A drink, maybe, to give one courage (6)
24 A vice that won't work? (2, 4)
26 Broken reed in which there's nothing to wear away (5)

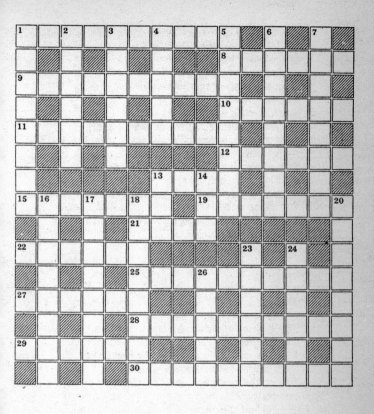

60

Across

1 Detectives return a ring in metal, in a manner of speaking (7)
5 The scene of an appeal against young Valentine? (4)
9 Alternative engine to a V8 rear-mounted, without any complications (15)
10 Simple lazy people take it so (4)
11 A dishy running partner! (5)
12 Look in a log lean-to (4)
15 He wanders around with foot in a towel (7)
16 Corresponded successfully with the marriage bureau? (7)
17 Quotes touchy point (7)
19 It has an enormous bill substituted in place (7)
21 Pull of old penny paper (4)
22 What one may possibly do when very pale (5)
23 It passes round the hat in more ways than one (4)
26 Nine detected by the breath test? (3, 4, 3, 5)
27 Does it mean wintry weather? Yes, except in Devon and Cornwall, apparently (4)
28 Graduates indeed valued less (7)

Down

1 Did, holding a machine gun, react to pressure from inside (7)
2 Peter, James, John, for instance? (9, 5)
3 Bloomer in which a pupil is to be found (4)
4 Pessimist who is a complete write-off (2-5)
5 Not on the bench and not up to the mark (3, 4)
6 Are they put on by pretentious disc-jockeys? (4)
7 It adds colour to a base Communist initiative (3, 4)
8 What practising campanologists did to relieve the monotony (4, 3, 7)
13 Frenchman leaves mother for someone else (5)
14 Writing instrument developed by a writer (5)
17 Tiresome little boy supported by letters of credit (7)
18 Bird which may fight and quarrel (7)
19 Nipped and nicked (7)
20 Not dead but tangled and knotted (7)
24 Where the heat is turned on in Coventry (4)
25 Cook uses a bit of her basil, for instance (4)

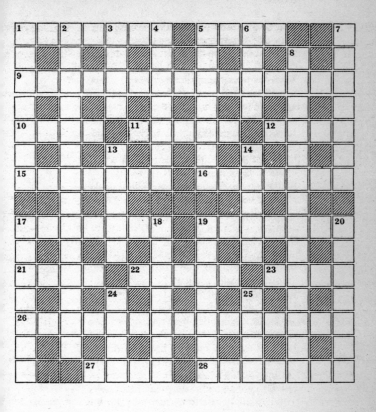

61

Across

1 Frankfurter selling fast at the races? (3, 9)
8 Girl has form above average (7)
9 Feelings expressed by small river birds (7)
11 And in a lover's embrace it goes to one's head (7)
12 Look the desert beast has swallowed medicine (7)
13 Route modified beyond what is acceptable (5)
14 They are services for all and sundry (3, 9)
16 Place to wine me in a state, oddly enough (9)
19 Enigmatic model (5)
21 Tool of proverbial attachment to a worker (7)
23 I follow the bird with an old rifle (7)
24 Uniform for a man in the Services (7)
25 A character in Arden or territory bounded by nothing (7)
26 Hooked the property-owning classes? (6, 6)

Down

1 Brazil, for example, when it comes to getting cracking (4, 3)
2 Triple Army unit's galley (7)
3 Place for a quiet tackle on Dartmoor (9)
4 He recorded a palpable hit in *Hamlet* (5)
5 Dress for a single drink on return (7)
6 Mother's upset it! (7)
7 Have a concerted bash to raise money? (4, 8)
10 The only fish that got away? (4, 8)
15 Off the cuff, so to speak (9)
17 Small figure giving colour to an Indian city (7)
18 Thought about numbers naturally having the means to move (7)
19 Chaucerian Dame not wholly occupied? (7)
20 Arboreal feature of a local encircled by a Scottish river (7)
22 Pistol's oyster globe (5)

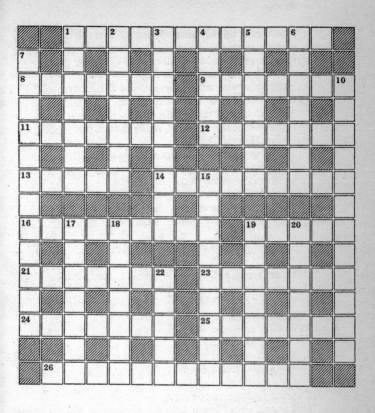

62

Across

1 They call loudly for change in public places (9)
9 A permit arranged for a high-ranking churchman (7)
10 Here, though in sad array, doesn't come unstuck (7)
11 A border cut by a mean figure (7)
12 Definitive version of *Dombey and Son*? (3, 3, 3)
14 His praises are sung in the services (8)
15 Not in robust health we hear, every so often (6)
17 They swoop down on fish, putting S.O.S. out about their victims (7)
20 Foolish person holding fixed property (6)
23 Disreputable solicitor from the Kent coast stating what the cards have to be (5, 3)
25 Putting on a picket at the farm? (9)
26 Contrasting points in a characteristic passage (7)
27 A take-off the tender-hearted Rodolfo couldn't bear to see! (7)
28 Lie that may get a backward pupil through an examination (7)
29 Dramatic alias? (5-4)

Down

2 & 3 Cry of surprise from desperate German minister in currency crisis! (3, 4, 3, 4)
4 Stayed with us erratically, coming at 15 across intervals (8)
5 Turns out to have a game on board (6)
6 One needs it for toast (4-5)
7 Salvation Army girl of great importance once in the Holy Land (7)
8 Serving-men who leave without giving notice (9)
13 Unorthodox poet clutching a period work (7)
15 Book written by Scott in a timber-yard? (9)
16 A home lost in a way that arouses disgust (9)
18 Edward Heath's main interest outside politics (8)
19 He gave superb lectures on current affairs (7)
21 Are nibs like this found in Belgrade? (7)
22 Display of temper from an abstainer fuddled with drink (7)
24 Makes a speech and gives out notes? (6)

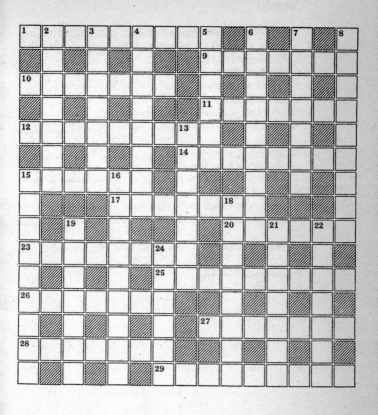

63

Across

1 Where a child would have needed fifty languages? (5)
4 A fielder who would presumably slow up the runs (5-3)
10 Television band between England and France (7)
11 Discovered a pound may be obtained honestly (7)
12 A spot of refreshment restored in the Middle East (4)
13 What the reporter wants to dig out (5)
14 How one should be even if right in a way (4)
17 Bargain hurriedly made by a Faustian tanner? (4, 3, 7)
19 It indicates the proper course prescribed by a school for models (7, 7)
22 China lacks a prominent feature (4)
23 The careful builder knows an accurate one reads the same both ways (5)
24 Hand is to be found in the foot (4)
27 Chastise a domestic animal, in particular a dog (7)
28 Trout is dished up for the hotel guest, perhaps (7)
29 Household supporters who get others into various habits (8)
30 Father went first, but showed some sign of fright (5)

Down

1 It pains one who stoops to give support to a revolutionary figure (8)
2 It bores an American lawyer caught in a vulgar fight (7)
3 Advanced forty days (4)
5 React fearfully – before taking the plunge? (4, 4, 6)
6 Travel around the Eternal City by the sound of it (4)
7 Descent of the shipping company era (7)
8 Irresponsibly heading for a fall? (5)
9 To vote for king supported by one dishonest person may currently raise the temperature (8, 6)
15 Previously the first vowel in place of the second (5)
16 Was it used for punishing back-parts? (5)
18 What the demonstrators did when shaken (8)
20 Opening suggestion that conditions may alternatively be freezing (7)
21 The first capital, no doubt (7)

63

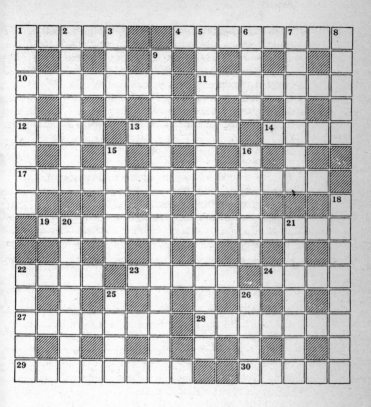

22 The colonel, having married, no longer shows any fight (5)
25 Vegetable liquids rise where mineral waters do, too (4)
26 Refuse tip of the French politician (4)

131

64

Across

1 Occasion when victory must be won in a great hurry (2, 4, 2, 4)
8 They protect X when commendatory gestures are about (7)
9 Specific cure that takes some licking! (7)
11 Star player offering four to one in new role (7)
12 Less ornate sort of praline (7)
13 Cosy feature of a mountain glen (5)
14 The flower that reposes on the best dairyman's sideboard? (9)
16 Eastern farm animal that is not heartless, but full of enthusiasm (9)
19 County councillor going round as a sour conspirator (5)
21 Foreign-made goods I'm bearing South (7)
23 A pledge not to be regarded lightly (7)
24 The range of sound being talked about? (7)
25 Brisk direction for noted bars (7)
26 The end of friendship? (12)

Down

1 Achieving his aim, the footballer may shake it! (7)
2 Cornish industrial establishment where there has always been under-employment (3, 4)
3 Wild bear breaking into wry smile, though far from happy (9)
4 Kind of bulb to recommend about the middle of July (5)
5 The ancestry of the railway era? (7)
6 Cast in a very bad shape (7)
7 The other team that Hamlet could always see? (8, 4)
10 Picture story that reveals all maybe! (5, 7)
15 Early leaf of nominal importance (5-4)
17 Some strikers cannot be dismissed without their agreement (7)
18 Wiggly curl on a lady's dog (7)
19 A recoil perplexes her (7)
20 Cunning Solicitor at Law with two pairs of braces! (7)
22 Student protest – and what is wrong about it (3-2)

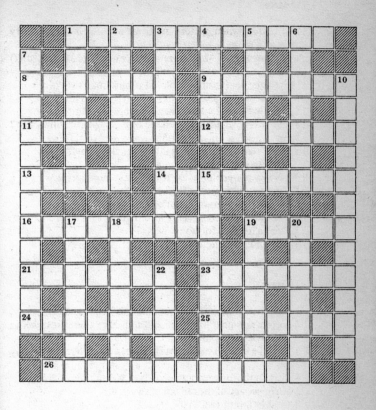

65

Across

6 Sacked! In fact, fired like a shot (10)
8 A friend to make much of (4)
9 A Lawrence goes into the affair at a nursery tea-party (3, 6)
11 A, B, C, D, F, G. Any one of them (4)
12 Abstainer swallows nothing but a very small drink (3)
13 For land workers, an attempt to start vegetables (9)
16 Broom with 19 down wouldn't be much use for cleaning it (4)
17 A parish priest and archbishop show approval (7)
18 On the warm side, presumably, so simmer down (4, 3)
20 Small piece of wood – pine (4)
21 Nervous analysis? (9)
23 Spoil the upset butter (3)
24 Study pointed geometrical figure (4)
25 One named for the post (9)
29 Beat the unbeatable (4)
30 Ferry often mishandled with sheer impudence (10)

Down

1 Company not in a state of liquidation? (4)
2 Sort of electricity I had expected to find in a car battery (4)
3 Mother of highly educated twins? (4)
4 It enters a gate to create a disturbance (7)
5 Fair run-off arranged with no money stakes (4, 3, 3)
7 Job for a navvy at the crossroads? (5, 4)
8 Carlton somehow has to find a singer (9)
10 The man's in this (3)
13 Notes left for the delivery boy? (5, 5)
14 Plot an assignment (9)
15 Foreshadow a literally unspeakable speed (9)
19 Intercept an order from the Queen of Hearts (4, 3)
22 The underworld boss young Sidney's backing (3).
26 Once enough to upset W.1 (4)
27 Sound vision is needed for building on (4)
28 Country I have entered before (4)

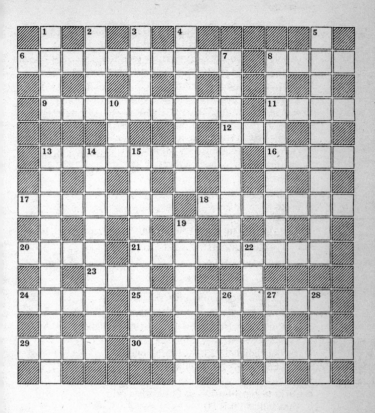

66

Across

7 Gets on a horse in a remote part of Cornwall (6, 3)
8 New York girl installed as a child minder (5)
10 Apply to get up in fort, possibly (3, 2, 3)
11 A calling held by the civil engineer to be too servile (6)
12 Not far from a marine arsenal (4)
13 Carry on an unauthorised procedure? (2, 3, 3)
15 Put in quarantine, 21 down haphazardly took a meal (7)
17 Mood of abstraction I outwardly respect (7)
20 Move around to secure a sailor's dismissal? (3, 5)
22 A case that is hard to try (4)
25 Nevertheless, a huge swimmer comes to no conclusion about it (6)
26 A carpet I refashioned for some financial consideration (2, 1, 5)
27 They naturally cover relations on board (5)
28 Just short of farce that isn't highly entertaining? (3, 6)

Down

1 Discredited solo trumpeter, maybe! (5)
2 Unit circling a wood and blazing away (2, 4)
3 Invite trouble for appearing in a piece of light satire (3, 3, 2)
4 It stops gunners going in slow-moving craft (7)
5 But for one misplaced note he might be a fine vocalist! (8)
6 Baffling breed of giant mice (9)
9 A Northerner who provides company in a way (4)
14 Stars of the publishing world (9)
16 Securing a dog a bone in its natural setting (8)
18 Recent disturbance about an actor's appearance (8)
19 Small thanks both ways, lad, can serve as encouragement in the States (7)
21 Makes things easier for artistic requirements (4)
23 No need to do so when one has a thousand in bonus shares! (6)
24 Bills I'd put in for etching requisites (5)

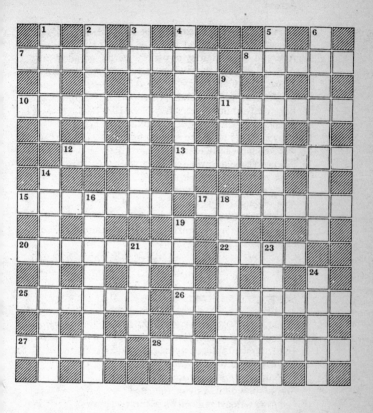

67

Across

1 Oxfordshire landmark noted for a fine beringed equestrienne (7, 5)
9 A sound chance outlay or one furthering no good purpose (7)
10 Concerning a lean objective thinker (7)
11 Cover, love, for Adriatic bathers (4)
12 Repeatedly one to profit (5)
13 Give a twist to music-hall entertainment (4)
16 Protean actor holds degree as a nimble performer (7)
17 The last places where travellers are likely to be met (7)
18 If so disposed, can then bewitch (7)
21 Reducing to tears? Splendid! (7)
23 Being a varied diet, it fluctuates (4)
24 Alias James, burglarious assistant (5)
25 Favourable for sale of goods (4)
28 To lie once more about pedigree (7)
29 Like a leader of pride (7)
30 Carroll adventurer? Wells, too – in the outback (5, 7)

Down

1 Second-rate pawnbroker should be a good mixer (7)
2 Initially an uprising to form defensive organisation (4)
3 The kind of attitude expected of one subject to 8 down (7)
4 He picked the white for royal preference (7)
5 Of genuine value no more in Spain (4)
6 Incentives limit us when readjusted (7)
7 & 8 House rule invoked for the suspension of sittings? (13, 8, 5)
14 Honour? Ah! It's sorcery! (5)
15 Supports playful chattels (5)
19 Afterthought by one with the will to change (7)
20 Not those superior to us who conquered the Amazon (7)
21 Desultory walker confined to the garden? (7)
22 Characters with a leaning to the right (7)
26 Record is held by District of Columbia (4)
27 Flyer's under-cover in Ireland (4)

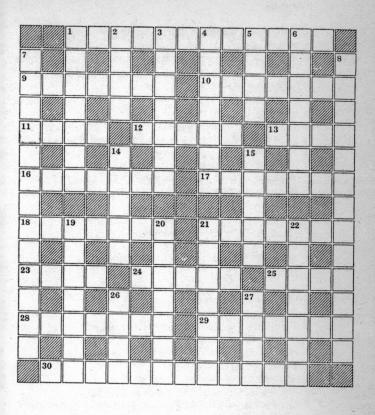

67

68

Across

1 Skate on ice? But he's far too aloof and unfriendly (4, 4)
5 Take steps to protect someone (6)
9 Something easily done when the offensive is complete (4-4)
10 Vehicle going round Middle East with a vital piece of TV equipment (6)
11 Dishevelled rover given broken pie that should have been eaten before (8)
12 What the fishmonger and his wares have in common (6)
14 Map letters designed to help the benighted traveller (6, 4)
18 The men who fix the rates of course! (4-6)
22 One type of fan club (6)
23 They charge a county council with devious ruses (8)
24 Badly dressed fellows quietly put into smart turn-out (6)
25 It's how far I'd reverse the position taken up (8)
26 Not footmen recommended by prudent jurymen? (6)
27 Averse to doing anything not lined out (8)

Down

1 One who has taken cover on a rocky height (6)
2 Bound to be cruelly treated (6)
3 Farinaceous see consumed by violent anger (6)
4 It's a lucky person who can make a profit out of it (10)
6 Notedly abrupt cats climbing over another from Man? (8)
7 Put on too much weight (8)
8 A wing consisting of ten parts (8)
13 Not a direct form of calumny or slander (10)
15 She cannot see those who call for her assistance (8)
16 Wild colt in desert country (8)
17 Unseemly person who lassoes a goblin? (8)
19 Those well-known stories? Precisely! (4, 2)
20 Its members are prepared to hear beyond grave news (6)
21 Lay claim to a lock-up (6)

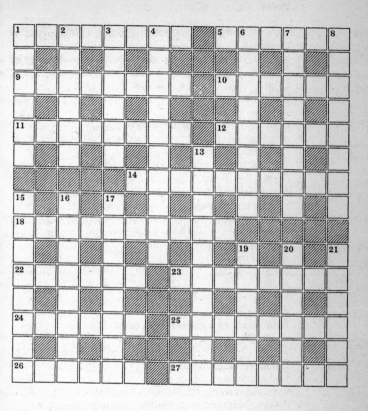

69

Across

1 Home's successor is about right for Home's familiar precursor (6)
4 Was apparently flashy sled going round the country house grounds (8)
9 Figure it might be an anaesthetic (6)
10 Declare wrongly the winner of the gallery's beauty contest? (8)
12 Does its music go round and around? (4)
13 About 10 fine beers do really need bush (5)
14 Be a Frenchman and put on a bright smile (4)
17 Church service which provides small scope for clerics (6, 6)
20 In wild desire I still find sources of fiery spirit (12)
23 Vegetable discovered when ship's bottom is turned over (4)
24 Soft cry of pain produces purse, but not of the lips (5)
25 Jewish priest of evil disposition (4)
28 The emblem of progress which increasingly only stands in all our ways (5-3)
29 Frequently seen it was, especially before the Enclosure Acts (6)
30 Unhappy Italian leader pointed to a sectarian of days gone by (8)
31 Pronounced 12 across to be proscribed (6)

Down

1 Extremity on account of a little advertising matter (8)
2 An old fossil, seemingly a worshipper of a ram-headed god (8)
3 Drew the sort of house which may be the property of 20 across (4)
5 Priority shown by the snobbish resident? (5, 2, 5)
6 Get up a union demand (4)
7 Editorial chief (6)
8 Aspirations represented by the same doctor (6)
11 Descriptive of those who contrive to tie on extra (12)
15 Los Angeles, in evil, now no more (5)
16 It needs a driver to enter the wood (5)

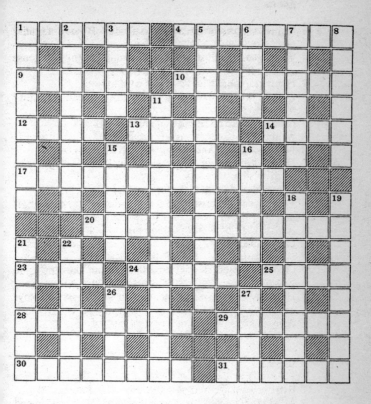

18 Main electricity worker who sometimes calls in and sometimes calls out (8)
19 Detailed description of document in its originally executed form (8)
21 Many arms and legs have been broken during them (6)
22 Watered unwanted plant dry in the middle (6)
26 Language used in four durbars (4)
27 It may be produced by carbon monoxide to some degree (4)

Across

8 Rotter returns a Postal Order, giving instruction to repeat notes from the beginning (2, 4)
9 Gratifying request to perform as a vocalist (8)
10 Do they reproduce the spirit of the picture? (6)
11 From a Greek island, first-class return brings you to Africa (8)
12 Advice to people ordering tea (3)
13 Encouraging suggestion from a yacht owner to his guests? (4, 2)
14 Paid attention to the three-line whip, apparently (8)
16 Studied replacement of one by 500 with lots of bosses (7)
18 Quietly tell a story to a high churchman (7)
23 Wave around chicken-feed container? (8)
27 Suffolk ness which can be reached other than by a bridge (6)
28 A branch of the Services – a commando-like one in particular (3)
29 Amorous sign of Claudius's nervousness? (8)
30 Chinese Communist article inside anything but dry (6)
31 Cab bill I tear to pieces according to inspired authority (8)
32 What primitively equipped boy anglers do for sartorial ornament (3-3)

Down

1 The Army's final call which put an end to the day of mail (4, 4)
2 Tyneside town Berliners would welcome (8)
3 Seven points containing nothing but sheer stupidity (8)
4 He was tough enough to fight and beat (7)
5 Extract an eviction order (3, 3)
6 Like a sea-bird behind the ship (6)
7 Somewhat later, but nevertheless punctual (2, 4)
15 Seven Poles leave the day before (3)
17 The sort of cheque which may be returned all the same (3)
19 Boarding companion gives accommodation to a ship's officer (4-4)
20 Not used to being right under? (4-4)

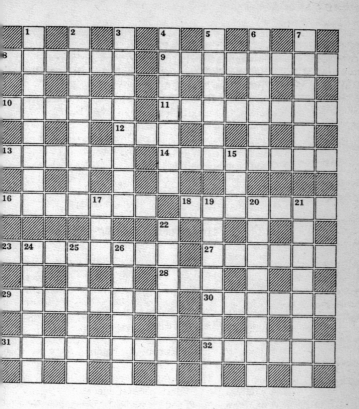

1 It gives a roasting, and turns on mine (8)
2 He lacks contrivance for restricting foot movement (7)
4 Castle that is a new one in force (6)
5 A quarter betimes, almost (6)
6 Where lies the art of diplomacy unimpaired (6)

71

Across

1 Impressive work in which all countries are represented (5, 5)
6 Discharges a liability, and still shows a profit (4)
9 A flower to cultivate in a celibate institution (10)
10 Heroic tale of Southern Turkish commander (4)
13 A girl ushered around, and not allowed to roam at will (7)
15 Literary man making hot soup in a very old city (6)
16 She swam divinely (6)
17 Talented person who goes out to make a scene (9, 6)
18 Gets ready to run lots of coaches together (6)
20 Good writers won't do this (6)
21 Not well away from the coast? (7)
22 Reactionary observation on the Thames (4)
25 The going price for a bachelor diet? (6, 4)
26 Slight quarrel, though it turns very noisy (4)
27 Batting No. 11 with foot trouble, but managing to surviv (7, 3)

Down

1 If we go out she's in charge of the house (4)
2 Revile the system of 18 across (4)
3 Fourth-rate current club (6)
4 A boon to the marksman who cannot get close to hi target (10, 5)
5 Song-writers who rise high in their profession? (6)
7 A wildly acclaimed university product (10)
8 A man who is good and yet makes progress impossible (10)
11 The way in which the American stock-market operate (4, 6)
12 Keep well away from an old and a soft medley (5, 5)
13 Sort of loss one doesn't restrain (7)
14 Lad who may go over well (7)
19 In the main nothing turns up for her (6)
20 Prevent others from seeing a riddle? (6)
23 Whip-round for the old censor (4)
24 They support line divisions (4)

Across

6 Did you win, darling? Apparently not, as between bitter
  rivals (2, 4, 4)
8 Backward servant on the old farm (4)
9 He conducted the opera twice in reverse (9)
11 Look both ways (4)
12 Number that is an imposture (3)
13 After the South African province came into being? (4-5)
16 Old advice bringing colour to the East (4)
17 Exult about an Irish author, we hear (7)
18 Flower to an American, but another to a Scot (7)
20 Best round to Bobby (4)
21 Retreat constructed by an oysterman (9)
23 Poor player, sliced between slices? (3)
24 An affirmative in Spain has a following in this part of the
  globe (4)
25 Healthy practices that could present problems (9)
29 Go home like Gray's ploughman (4)
30 Articles maybe, though steps would be novel (6-4)

Down

1 An automatic runner of course (4)
2 Decorations which are often fiddled (4)
3 Letter 20 garbled (4)
4 Giant oil mix-up in his homeland (7)
5 A burning passion leads him to destruction (10)
7 Iron still capable of making vast sums (9)
8 An obvious exaggeration from the Greek over a tree-trunk
  (9)
10 Suggestion of censorship in an Homeric utterance (3)
13 Ernie helps in a way, being capable of grasping (10)
14 Signs of the small worker (9)
15 Laconic remark that amounts to nothing (2, 7)
19 Meantime, bury him in Cockney style (7)
22 Japanese fish, it is recalled, with a heart (3)
26 Important enough to be something in it? (4)
27 & 28 Where an encore made a transatlantic stir? (4, 4)

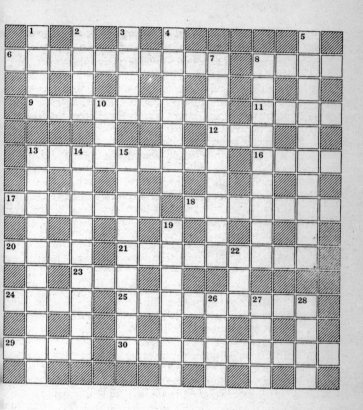

Across

6 It adds distinction to the case for strikers (5-3, 5)
8 Backward places or the lethargy they produce (6)
9 It could be a view that is openly conveyed (8)
10 Something nailed from the West? (3)
11 The rim of an iron-bound hoop (6)
12 Straggling deserts I fought against (8)
14 Burnt out residue is swallowed by His Highness as a drug (7)
16 Fish put on when wine is about (7)
20 Dining at resort, the non-abstainer may call for one (3, 3, 2)
23 A man who heals with pointed instruments and speaks slowly (6)
24 Loch that commands respect (3)
25 A trusty arrangement about a sculptural work (8)
26 Carry on with the summary (6)
27 Made to play into a cunning adversary's hands? (6, 2, 1, 4)

Down

1 A faucet put on a small island, if need be (2, 1, 5)
2 Contracts out of anguish or tension (8)
3 He acts as a link-man in show business (7)
4 They secure quiet when the form is outside (6)
5 It's quite simply a computer (6)
6 Incapable of forgetting things? (13)
7 A plan that goes into a lot of detail (5-5, 3)
13 Poetic land of discordant din (3)
15 Alpine flower that doesn't close until late at night (3)
17 Civic dignitary would appear to be arboreal (8)
18 Address required by more than one businessman (4, 4)
19 Doesn't sally forth to check wrong-doing (5, 2)
21 A king badly hurt, the hero of many a legend (6)
22 A weight card returned to the Queen (6)

73

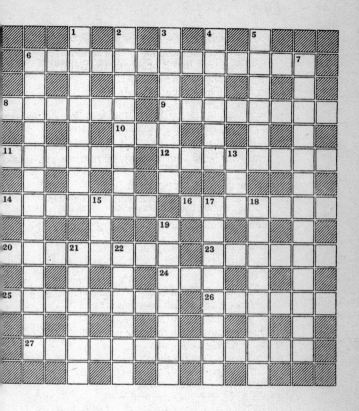

151

74

Across

1 He probably remembers El Alamein as a waste before the sailor's return (6, 3)
9 In occupational outlay the object becomes a matter of habit (7)
10 Fellow allowed a wreath (7)
11 Girl in a tale unusually written (7)
12 Given accommodation divided into four (9)
14 Incidentally, where hitch-hikers may be seen (2, 3, 3)
15 Seer to create a sort of record (6)
17 A man of the type who employed a devil (7)
20 Doges upset about a spirit they might aptly have worshipped (3-3)
23 Dull description of a play producer's position (8)
25 Is it for detecting the presence of fairies all the way round (9)
26 I'd turn to poetry just to be different (7)
27 In which Eastern fathers hold a figure to worship? (7)
28 Apparently no clubs or spades are included as arms for Ulster (3, 4)
29 The sort of job which gives one little standing (9)

Down

2 Waste of petrol and tire (7)
3 Rome rep. in a way! (7)
4 The reformist is not fogged archaically on that account (8)
5 Finish in an attempt to be with it (6)
6 The county which droops before the price of service (9)
7 Babylonian idol makes a sound like a cow. No, like a bull (7)
8 Balance which will be in the red if iron-workers strike (9)
13 One bite breaks vulcanised rubber (7)
15 Not primary measure of time needed before ray disperses (9)
16 He loved the pleasures of heroic poetry and a rune deciphered (9)
18 Roughly calculate new tea times (8)
19 Deprave, upset, and extend influence through everything (7)
21 Herb has the price of a drink (7)

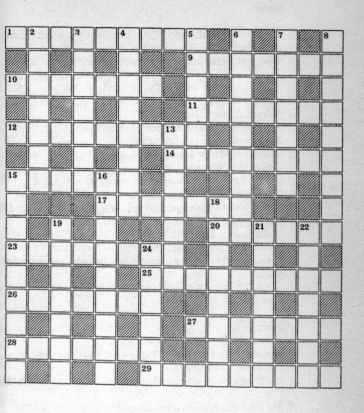

22 Begin with a tune outside (4, 3)
24 Objects to the final odds, but still gets rid of money (6)

75

Across

1 Kind set in printing (4)
3 Beyond the fifth letter, a sticky application (5)
6 How travellers journey in an endless safari (4)
11 Study how to cause a blackout muddle (7)
12 A colourful trap for the cocktail party (4, 3)
13 He may not get his baccalaureate should he fail to put in enough degree marks (13)
16 As in religious belief in need of pressing (7)
17 Pair 2 with an unidentified quantity (7)
18 There is probably a pile in it, but show some response to an alternative (7)
21 It would be a trifle heavy for a writing-tablet clasp (7)
23 Despondent revelation of the cardiograph? (5-8)
26 Where lads may be sent if returning to rob, a last resort (7)
27 Not in time, hurried to a Roman church (7)
28 Swelling only five notes of the scale apparently (4)
29 By holding and with legs bent (5)
30 Concern of the vice squad, ambassador, and politician (4)

Down

1 It may reduce the waist of the dress, but not of the wearer (4)
2 In coins an ecclesiastical fine (7)
4 Got one's own back even though old and venerable within (7)
5 Nautical term used by prime minister in after-dinner speech (7)
7 Footballers arrived at something to play (7)
8 It needs time-keepers to do so (4)
9 How to get solution which is purest as a true interpretation (13)
10 Failing to show respect when sailing below the surface over the line (13)
14 Cut and run? (5)
15 County sounds inhuman (5)
19 Swore that a number made a mistake (7)
20 A parrot took to the air and the whole lot goes up (7)
21 Drunk for keeps? (7)

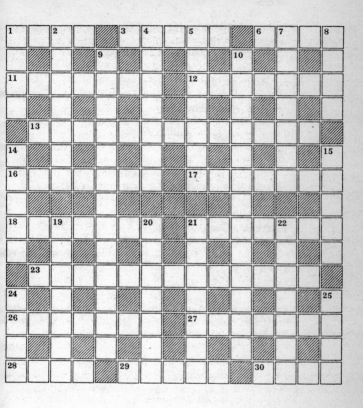

22 Comment, see? (7)
24 Resort educated man enters on Scottish tour (4)
25 A call for the same cards (4)

76

Across

1 Weighing up the arguments for reimposing military occupation? (12)
8 A heron's resort on the Yorkshire coast (7)
9 Injunction one cannot go and obey (4, 3)
11 A mastic tree? Let's ink in the answer! (7)
12 Genuine ingredient of foods in cereal form (7)
13 Starts to write in circles (5)
14 What I demand when I can't find my seat! (5, 2, 2)
16 It guards against the risks of a sudden falling off in performance (6, 3)
19 A table bird in top gear, apparently (5)
21 Was in store for, at a wide adjustment (7)
23 Men restraining a wild set of most illiberal character (7)
24 The better half of a pocket-size ruler (7)
25 French painter I continually grumble about (7)
26 Exceptionally strong punch? (5-3, 4)

Down

1 It cruelly restricts and has been called vile (7)
2 False allegations about a fool of whom Burns wrote with great admiration (7)
3 Negroes of unhealthy appearance rarely encountered in Australia (5, 4)
4 Small river snakes that grate on the ears (5)
5 New Aintree apprentice (7)
6 Wearing result of being deprived of forty winks (7)
7 Pretty well all Snug had! (3, 5, 4)
10 Attractive sales offer that's a pleasure to look forward to? (5, 2, 5)
15 Ten items a French café concocted (9)
17 Take a rise out of apartment No. 11's neighbour (7)
18 Huge 24 across coming to a different conclusion (7)
19 Something one has to allow in retrospect after informal conversation (7)
20 Quietly criticise a Press showing (7)
22 One in hand raised nothing for some stars (5)

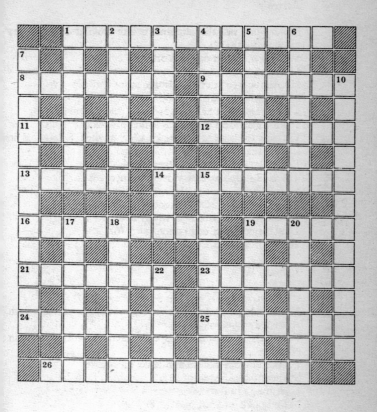

77

Across

8 Maybe one of a chequered board making a firework display (3, 5)
9 Support armed robbery (4, 2)
10 Does but one (3)
11 He's the sort who is always looking for a way in, a way out, and alternative! (8)
12 Cleric's assurance that the poor dog had a meal (6)
13 Traitorously cash in on land values? (4, 4, 7)
15 Fitting in the first to murder an army officer (7)
18 Executes advice given to ambitious young teachers (7)
21 Refugee moved up one in the queue (9, 6)
24 Travelling archaeologist's cry when eager for Chaldean study? (2, 4)
25 Ideas notwithstanding, the setback of a pious soul (8)
26 Witchcraft Robin takes to heart (3)
27 They may be realised in group form (6)
28 With which the artist labours, suffering in chaotic toil (3-5)

Down

1 Medium demonstration with a spirited sit-down? (6)
2 Ask for a soft chime of bells (6)
3 Teaching the lesson tennis learners find most difficult? (7, 2, 6)
4 Put on different clothes and make up (7)
5 Successful candidates in Israeli elections? (3, 6, 6)
6 Nightingale in Italy (8)
7 Many spoke, but not plainly (8)
14 Thirsty greyhounds do one circuit of the course (3)
16 A falsehood isn't confusing to a psychiatrist (8)
17 Lists bad news for waiters (4, 4)
19 Fool, by heading off the mass (3)
20 No, it is up to males to make a remark (7)
22 Overcoat made from old cloth, pound article (6)
23 Two ways one can pass through a door, note, for a short journey (6)

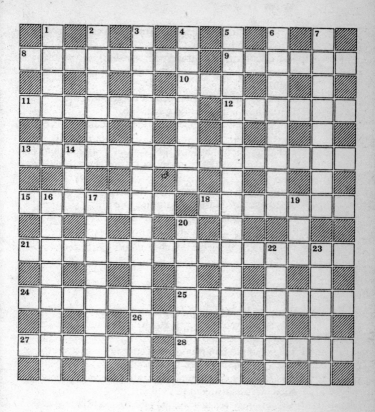

78

Across

1 In no condition to act, so came to a fresh arrangement (8)
5 It ran around mortified (6)
9 Individual copies returned with speed (8)
10 Pleased about being brought in, though looked far from it! (6)
11 Neatly conclude a postponed club game? (5, 3)
12 Dormant fish turned into a snake (6)
14 Not the first ex-Prime Minister to define a weekend cottage! (6, 4)
18 Debating point that cannot be conducive to harmony (10)
22 In their moment of triumph they sank beneath the waves (1-5)
23 Heather goes after another girl for a Tory politician (8)
24 Small band of Marines in strange tale (6)
25 It may strengthen or weaken an army . . . (8)
26 . . . to engage in its service (6)
27 A spot of comfort for the local visitor (8)

Down

1 One who has benefited from America's troubles (6)
2 Maybe one needs to get this to plan the proceedings in detail (3, 3)
3 Traffic-bound unit producing a string of invective! (6)
4 Essential equipment for the consumer? (3, 2, 5)
6 A friend with odd ideas for stakes (8)
7 Attacked and made to run? (6, 2)
8 A diver or bather interrupted by an American lawyer (8)
13 Natural hue that makes one pass over the ceremonial speech (10)
15 Precise bill supported by a junior minister (8)
16 Unpretentious bench with half a bent nail at each end (8)
17 They don't believe he requires capital in Greece (8)
19 Having nothing particular to do, I'd fish (6)
20 In a penalty it is of limited significance (6)
21 A representative business (6)

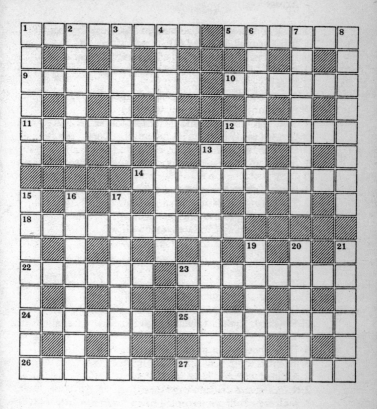

Across

3 Loudly simulates authentic data (5)
8 & 9 Irregular work for part-time Socialism (6, 6)
10 Barn-stormer going round all West Riding parishes (6)
11 Puts in different classes of pop players (8)
12 Half sleep in the nursery (3)
13 Base move to cover a sovereign fortress (6)
14 A bet torn up among none, take note (4, 4)
17 & 19 Stronghold over the hill? Lie low (4, 3, 2, 5)
23 Girl with Roman garment for travel in New York (8)
27 Re-styled robe on a spritely monarch (6)
29 Suitable address for an officer (3)
30 Somehow Simon had to issue a warning (8)
31 Noted French studies (6)
32 Five score see the order to dress (6)
33 Craft worker at the tailor's (6)
34 Cooking facility for the cowhand (5)

Down

1 Fruity Zola heroine undergraduate (6)
2 Period of a sentence (4, 4)
3 A wicked device, made light of (8)
4 & 22 Shocking style of those in the swim? (7, 7)
5 Not much of an insult (6)
6 To incorporate a sailor's world (6)
7 Mashed turnip held up stage proceedings (6)
13 & 24 'Dost thou think, because thou art virtuous, there shall be no more — — — ?' (*Twelfth Night*, Act 2) (5, 3, 3)
15 A steamer, stupid! (3)
16 Consumed a quarter on erupting Etna (5)
18 Make choice tea (sound suggestion!) after work (3)
20 The girl Dante was forced to leave (8)
21 In the players' union it's not fair play (8)
22 See 4 down
24 See 13 down
25 Fosters advertisements about 18 down (6)
26 Organic invocation for Roland's comrade (6)

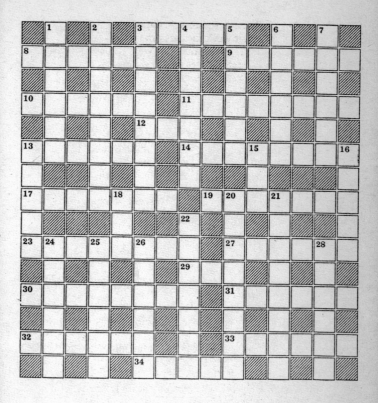

28 Daisy, when grown, may be entitled to the Junoesque epithet (2-4)

80

Across

8 At this spot an ambassador meets the Engineers (4)
9 The son of Noah avoided by orthodox Jews (3)
10 Centre of unrest given too much cover? (6)
11 A thousand get into a row and slander (6)
12 A sun tile designed to avoid extremes of temperature (8)
13 Unlike Queen Victoria, visit the comedy players (3, 3, 5, 4)
15 Strip that cartoonists do (4, 3)
17 Famous poet goes from bank to bank (7)
20 The whole story of the finished jig-saw (8, 7)
23 Left the Sahara, for instance, to little Edward (8)
25 Sick in bed, though named to appear (6)
26 Chased by the sound of it, but apparently managed to escape! (6)
27 A sensational success whichever way you look at it (3)
28 Mind the Kremlin's reply to a White House request? (4)

Down

1 Argument in which the young socialite was evidently sustained (6)
2 Scorn advice to eschew ambition? (8)
3 With it, each wet fog an indisposition brought to her (6, 2, 7)
4 Irreligious little devil with debts (7)
5 Pursuing dreams in the hopes of finding potted gold? (7, 8)
6 List in a vessel providing one with higher standing (6)
7 Fingered heavy fabric (4)
14 What the martyr will do can make an impression (3)
16 Past what the impatient competitor wants (3)
18 Origin of article which may cause travellers the loss of a day (4-4)
19 Fail to lower (3, 4)
21 Polite request when a sleep is disturbed (6)
22 He enters USSR compound to get a monkey (6)
24 The lingering note in a fine chorus (4)

80

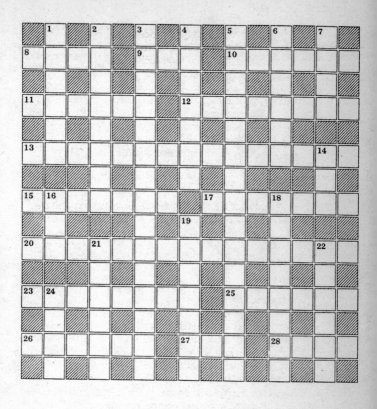

165

Solutions

No. 1
Across. – 1, Habitant; 5, Peewit; 9, Manifest; 10, Splint; 11, Laureate; 12, Murcia; 14, Strike back; 18, Fleshlings; 22, Saturn; 23, Croaking; 24, Oporto; 25, Mediocre; 26, Taking; 27, Greyness.

Down. – 1, Homely; 2, Banquo; 3, Tuffet; 4, Nose to tail; 6, Espoused; 7, Whinchat; 8, Titlarks; 13, Ginger beer; 15, Offshoot; 16, Left hook; 17, Sheraton; 19 and 20, Family circle; 21, Egress.

No. 2
Across. – 1, Charity ball; 8, Bernardette; 11, Onus; 12, Elia; 13, Fellows; 15, Brioche; 16, Names; 17, Hour; 18, Area; 19, Homer; 21, Smarten; 22, Lebanon; 23, Lien; 26, Icon; 27, Auctioneers; 28, Black Forest.

Down. – 2, Hies; 3, Run down; 4, Turn; 5, Brewers; 6, Lyte; 7, Wolf-whistle; 8, Built-up area; 9, Electronics; 10, Gale warning; 14, Saxon; 15, Bevel; 19, Hepatic; 20, Red deer; 24, Null; 25, Loaf; 26, Iris.

No. 3
Across. – 7, Draw in one's horns; 8, Scatter; 10, Portion; 11, Rebut; 12, Mason; 14, Prime; 15, Sign; 16, Hold; 17, Shop; 19, Hasp; 21, Onset; 22, Harpy; 23, Pilot; 25, Steward; 26, Pastels; 27, Confidence trick.

Down. – 1, Procrastination; 2, Two twos; 3, Under; 4, Ascot; 5, Costard; 6, Endowment policy; 9, Rein; 10, Push; 13, Night; 14, Plush; 17, Sea-wife; 18, Paid; 19, Hoop; 20, Pattern; 23, Pride; 24, Tales.

No. 4
Across. – 1, Contour map; 6, Free; 10, Limed; 11, Dunce's cap; 12, Rearmost; 13, Reply; 15, Outlook; 17, Sceptre; 19, Nanette; 21, Retreat; 22, Chile; 24, Forfeits; 27, Enamoured; 28, Brook; 29, Pits; 30, Sea-serpent.

Down. – 1, Cold; 2, Number Ten; 3, Order; 4, Red-book; 5, Annates; 7, Recap; 8, Empty seats; 9, Bear left; 14, Going cheap; 16, On the dot; 18, Twenty-one; 20, Enforce; 21, Reredos; 23, Inapt; 25, Ember; 26, Skit.

No. 5

Across. – 1, Lovelace; 5, Pampas; 9, Soil-pipe; 10, In part; 11, Open-eyed; 12, Stater; 14, Chopsticks; 18, Tread water; 22, Enamel; 23, Addition; 24, Maimed; 25, Scenario; 26, Donate; 27, Assessor.

Down. – 1, Lesson; 2, Veiled; 3, Lapsed; 4, Copperhead; 6, Annotate; 7, Practice; 8, Satirist; 13, Appendices; 15, Streamed; 16, Relation; 17, Adherent: 19, Fiancé; 20, Mitres; 21, Indoor.

No. 6

Across. – 1, Scrap-book; 8, Repetitive job; 11, Fate; 12, Rings; 13, Isis; 16, Casting; 17, Sheathe; 18, Unstaid; 20, Service; 21, Soho; 22, Funny; 23, Skit; 26, Lift attendant; 27, Smartened.

Down. – 2, Crew; 3, Abiding; 4, Bridges; 5, Open; 6, Dentist's chair; 7, Loose thinking; 9, Off course; 10, Usherette; 14, Dinar; 15, Berry; 19, Doubter; 20, Sincere; 24, Stem; 25, Edge.

No. 7

Across. – 1, Sculptors; 9, Career; 10, Principal; 11, Mallet; 12, Menagerie; 13, Cheers; 17, Bye; 19, Malaria; 20, Retinue; 21, Rag; 23, Lappet; 27, Centre-bit; 28, Bottle; 29, Court case; 30, Eschew; 31, Mechanism.

Down. – 2, Carmen; 3, Linear; 4, Tailed; 5, Reality; 6, Parachute; 7, Well-meant; 8, Protested; 14, Small beer; 15, Slapstick; 16, Orderlies; 17, Bar; 18, Erg; 22, Acetone; 24, Starch; 25, Deacon; 26, Misses.

No. 8

Across. – 1, The land of Nod; 8, Adamant; 9, Pontiac; 11, Stellar; 12, Tea-rose; 13, Greet; 14, Albatross; 16, Matchless; 19, Aesop; 21, Newgate; 23, Explåin; 24, Yearned; 25, Italian; 26, Chesterfield.

Down. – 1, Trapeze; 2, Epaulet; 3, Altercate; 4, Depot; 5, Fondant; 6, Orinoco; 7, Passage-money; 10, Chess opening; 15, Bas-relief; 17, Towpath; 18, Hyaenas; 19, Appease; 20, Sea-bird; 22, Eddie.

No. 9

Across. – 6, State religion; 8, Miller; 9, Harvests; 10, Spa; 11, Kimono; 12, Perusing; 14, Agitate; 16, Step out; 20, War-dance; 23, Bricks; 24, Tie; 25, Starters; 26, Renown; 27, Real-life story.

Down. – 1, Mail-boat; 2, Bears out; 3, Perhaps; 4, Mirror; 5, Divers; 6, Sailing-master; 7, Not in luck's way; 13, Ure; 15, Ada; 17, Tuberose; 18, Paignton; 19, Sets off; 21, Dorsal; 22, Niello.

No. 10

Across. – 1, Mandoline; 8, Sounding-board; 11, None; 12, Flood; 13, Coco; 16, Existed; 17, Deduces; 18, Lighted; 20, Skipper; 21, Neon; 22, Smart; 23, Stop; 26, Assassination; 27, Challenge.

Down. – 2, Aunt; 3, Drilled; 4, Logwood; 5, Nook; 6, Counting-house; 7, Preoccupation; 9, Underline; 10, Conscript; 14, State; 15, Ad lib; 19, Damosel; 20, Strange; 24, Cash; 25, Stag.

No. 11

Across. – 6, Lieutenant; 8, Soho; 9, Loathsome; 11, Fume; 12, See 7 down; 13, Hampstead; 16, Wren; 17, Spandau; 18, Improve; 20, Riot; 21, Diagnosis; 23, Rod; 24, Ogle; 25, Open heart; 29 and 30, Take no interest.

Down. – 1, Dill; 2, Aura; 3, Leah; 4, Halogen; 5, Themselves; 7 and 12 across, The odd man out; 8, Soft words; 10, Top; 13, Hopping mad; 14, Monotreme; 15, Stand down; 19, Rarebit; 22, Ore; 26, Hate; 27, Acre; 28, Tass.

No. 12

Across. – 1, Gang warfare; 9, Cede; 10, Good in parts; 11, Left; 14, Booklet; 16, Caravan; 17, Easel; 18, Drop; 19, Otic; 20, Sexes; 22, Whereas; 23, Send out; 24, Till; 28, Brigantines; 29, Mate; 30, Radio signal.

Down. – 2, Ahoy; 3, Gods; 4, Aintree; 5, Flat; 6, Retrial; 7, Reservation; 8, Pertinacity; 12, Abide With Me; 13, Go to bed late; 15, Tales; 16, Ceres; 20, Samaria; 21, Seconds; 25, Ugli; 26, Ring; 27, Vera.

No. 13

Across. – 7, Fire-flies; 8, Sling; 10, Customer; 11, In pain; 12, Once; 13, El Dorado; 16, Rare; 18, Impulse; 20, Adipose; 22, Rake; 24, Devotion; 26, Glad; 29, Purest; 30, Hear hear; 31, Ruler; 32, Greenness.

Down. – 1, Pious; 2, Bent on; 3, Slumbers; 4, Terrier; 5, Claptrap; 6, Unkindest; 9, Mind; 14, Leak; 15, Impetuous; 17, Aero; 19, Unopened; 21, Degraded; 23, Anchors; 25, Iota; 27, Athens; 28, Balsa.

No. 14

Across. – 1, Graver; 4, Psalmist; 9, Orange; 10, Cracks up; 12, Note; 13, Devil; 14, Legs; 17, Weather chart; 20, Gossip column; 23, Axis; 24, Merry; 25, Acts; 28, Intrepid; 29, Hobart; 30, Moreover; 31, Shelve.

Down. – 1, Good news; 2, Away team; 3, Edge; 5, Straight part; 6, Luce; 7, Issued; 8, Typist; 11, Heart's desire; 15, Whoop; 16, Brood; 18, Pub crawl; 19, Anisette; 21, Radium; 22, Litter; 26, Reno; 27, Pooh.

No. 15

Across. – 5, Halter; 8, Peterman; 9, Plays on; 10, Reach; 11, Easterner; 13, Tenantry; 14, Margin; 17, Eon; 19, Zen; 20, Not all; 23, Roulette; 26, Final word; 28, Strut; 29, Fissure; 30, Moon-shot; 31, Indeed.

Down. – 1, Spirit; 2, Strains; 3, Archangel; 4, Barber; 5, Halftime; 6, Layer; 7, Esoteric; 12, Aye; 15, Analysing; 16, Position; 18, Old World; 21, Err; 22, Starchy; 24, Odds-on; 25, Estate; 27, Aisle.

No. 16

Across. – 1, Chorus-girls; 8, Middle class; 11, Bear; 12, Text; 13, Encased; 15, Senator; 16, Salad; 17, Vamp; 18, Gnat; 19, Bigot; 21, Take out; 22, Nuptial; 23, Rent; 26, Sure; 27, Good spirits; 28, Bearing down.

Down. – 2, Hair; 3, Riddles; 4, Shem; 5, Ill-used; 6, Lest; 7, Observatory; 8, Match-making; 9, Sententious; 10, Story-teller; 14, Davit; 15, Salon; 19, Builder; 20, Tutored; 24, Tome; 25, Open; 26, Stew.

No. 17

Across. – 8, Some; 9, Odo; 10, Trashy; 11, Palace; 12, Privates; 13, Trend of the times; 15, Candent; 17, Pot-herb; 20, Trick of the trade; 23, Half fare; 25, Fourth; 26, Repast; 27, Roc; 28, Ewer.

Down. – 1, Hot air; 2, Remained; 3, Come down to earth; 4, Towpath; 5, Strive for effect; 6, Malawi; 7, Shoe; 14, Err; 16, Air; 18, Hercules; 19, At heart; 21, Caftan; 22, Dotted; 24, Alec.

No. 18

Across. – 1 and 5, Circular letter; 9, Addition; 10, Spouts; 12, Grape-vine; 13, Nahum; 14, Ebon; 16, Spinner; 19, Finnish; 21, Stem; 24, Ozone; 25, Rio Grande; 27, Reeves; 28, Neat-herd; 29, Extols; 30, Syndrome.

Down. – 1 and 17, Change of course; 2, Redcap; 3, Untie; 4 and 20, Aeolian harp; 6, Expensive; 7, Touching; 8, Rosemary; 11 and 21, Sets store by; 15, Bridewell; 17, See 1 down; 18, Insolent; 20, See 4 down; 21, See 11 down; 22, Angelo; 23, Beadle; 26, Rated.

No. 19

Across. – 8, Domineer; 9, Nordic; 10, Eat; 11, Corsairs; 12, Houses; 13, Die with laughter; 15, Informs; 18, Apostle; 21, Protest marchers; 24, Gareth; 25, Unionist; 26, Ill; 27, Retake; 28, Set aside.

Down. – 1, Potosi; 2, Jigsaw; 3, Get into mischief; 4, Trestle; 5, In the Upper Fifth; 6, Draughts; 7, Sidereal; 14, Elf; 16, Narrates; 17, On the way; 19, Tie; 20, Impulse; 22, Honest; 23, Reside.

No. 20

Across. – 7, Filling out forms; 8, Rebound; 10, Praetor; 11, Early; 12, Angel; 14, Again; 15, Doit; 16, Turn; 17, Curt; 19, Moor; 21, Flies; 22, Nadir; 23, Pears; 25, Rattled; 26, Shot-gun; 27, Capital offences.

Down. – 1, Give oneself away; 2, Allowed; 3, Inane; 4, Story; 5, Foreign; 6, Imposing figures; 9, Daft; 10, Plot; 13, Lotus; 14, Arson; 17, Certain; 18, Tied; 19, Mars; 20, Ratting; 23, Petal; 24, Shift.

No. 21

Across. – 1, Above board; 9, Fine; 10, All the same; 11, Ablest; 12, Play-pen; 15, Set down; 16, Round; 17, Pubs; 18, Tito; 19, Tepid; 21, Russian; 22, Lambert; 24, Orange; 27, Overgrowth; 28, Ebon; 29, Four-seater.

Down. – 2, Bill; 3, Votary; 4, Breeder; 5, Adam; 6, Dreaded; 7, Give notice; 8, Letting out; 12, Paper money; 13, Ambassador; 14, Nomen; 15, Snail; 19, Take off; 20, Damages; 23, Baroda; 25, Jehu; 26, Stye.

No. 22

Across. – 6, Worldly wisdom; 8, Snicks; 9, Explicit; 10, Ian; 11, Coping; 12, Audience; 14, Majesty; 16, Sun-dial; 20, Conclave; 23, Dismal; 24, Rye; 25, Price cut; 26, Relate; 27, Evening prayer.

Down. – 1, Practice; 2, Odd sight; 3, Mycenae; 4, Pipped; 5, Admire; 6, Went on a course; 7, Main character; 13, Inn; 15, Sal; 17, Underarm; 18, Displays; 19, Vertigo; 21, Cocker; 22, Archie.

No. 23

Across. – 1, Scratch race; 9, Sten; 10, Concordance; 11, Apse; 14, Replays; 16, Singles; 17, Sight; 18, Volt; 19, Etui; 20, Get up; 22, Clipper; 23, Tall one; 24, Togo; 28, Breaking out; 29, Over; 30, All the world.

Down. – 2, Coop; 3, Arcs; 4, Carboys; 5, Ream; 6, Cockpit; 7, Stipulation; 8, Interstices; 12, Provocation; 13, Spelling-bee; 15, Sixer; 16, Shout; 20, General; 21, Pastime; 25, Bait; 26, Agio; 27, Bull.

No. 24

Across. – 1, Uniformed; 9, Armoire; 10, Stand up; 11, Sirloin; 12, Ill at ease; 14, Elevator; 15, Behest; 17, Heathen; 20, Aghast; 23, Serenade; 25, Editorial; 26, Immerse; 27, Titanic; 28, Overlie; 29, Day-dreams.

Down. – 2, Natalie; 3, Fanfare; 4, Roulette; 5, Damsel; 6, Improving; 7, Riposte; 8, Re-entrant; 13, Seethed; 15, Bad sailor; 16, Shangri-la; 18, East wind; 19, Crammer; 21, Herbage; 22, Stadium; 24, Deemed.

No. 25

Across. – 1, Strapping lad; 8, Unclean; 9, Dear Sir; 11, Tiniest; 12, Shellac; 13, Resin; 14, Relief map; 16, Portended; 19, Tacit; 21, Annates; 23, Seed-oil; 24, Leonine; 25, Robsart; 26, Underpayment.

Down. – 1, Seconds; 2, Roedean; 3, Punctured; 4, Indus; 5, Glad-eye; 6, Absalom; 7, Culture pearl; 10, Recapitulate; 15, Led astray; 17, Rangoon; 18, Entwine; 19, Tremble; 20, Coolant; 22, Sleep.

No. 26

Across. – 1, Damaged; 5, Catcher; 9, Against; 10, Beer mug; 11, Eider-down; 12, Roost; 13, Doric; 15, Overtaken; 17, Displayed; 19, Chair; 22, Stuff; 23, What's what; 25, Indoors; 26, Obverse; 27, Garotte; 28, Rest not.

Down. – 1, Dead-end; 2, Meander; 3, Goner; 4, Dittology; 5, Cabin; 6, Theoretic; 7, Hammock; 8, Right on; 14, Cold front; 16, Endeavour; 17, Dashing; 18, Sounder; 20, Acheron; 21, Retreat; 23, Waste; 24, Saves.

No. 27

Across. – 1, Docking; 5, Blondes; 9, Command of the sea; 10, Door; 11, Perch; 12, Trek; 15, Dithers; 16, Look-see; 17, Minerva; 19, Applied; 21, Town; 22, Dacca; 23, Agio; 26, Hardy characters; 27, Systems; 28, Stepson.

Down. – 1, Decoded; 2, Comforting words; 3, Iran; 4, Gadgets; 5, Bifocal; 6, Otho; 7, Distressing news; 8, Shackle; 13, Ferry; 14, Poppy; 17, Matches; 18, Apaches; 19, Accords; 20, Drops in; 24, Byre; 25, Acre.

No. 28

Across. – 1, Maid of honour; 8, Incense; 9, Mugwump; 12, Ends; 13, Barry; 14, Moor; 17, Dampier; 18, Stilton; 19, Ulysses; 22, Apparel; 24, Like; 25, Staff; 26, Flog; 29, Solomon; 31, Bandits; 32, Round the bend.

Down. – 1, Macadam; 2, Iona; 3, Open air; 4, Humerus; 5, Nags; 6, Ram; 7, Mixed doubles; 10, U-boat; 11, Phrenologist; 15, First; 16, Nippy; 20, Yokel; 21, Satinet; 22, Affable; 23, Rallied; 27, Amen; 28, Knee; 30, Our.

No. 29

Across. – 1, Fresh face; 9, Mirror; 10, In a tangle; 11, Eltham; 12, Carried on; 13, Burden; 17, Esk; 19, Iron out; 20, Indexed; 21, Act; 23, Bel Ami; 27, Ordinance; 28, Hurdle; 29, Villagers; 30, Vanish; 31, Pretender.

Down. – 2, Rental; 3, Satire; 4, Fenced; 5, Callous; 6, Girl guide; 7, Orthodoxy; 8, Promenade; 14, Misbehave; 15, Collaring; 16, Formalist; 17, Eta; 18, Kit; 22, Cartier; 24, Billet; 25, Margin; 26, Scarce.

No. 30

Across. – 1, Permanent way; 8, Out of it; 9, Darters; 11, Keeps on; 12, Profile; 13, Noted; 14, Nightfall; 16, Melanesia; 19, Sidon; 21, Docking; 23, Parties; 24, Largess; 25, Sun-dial; 26, Seven Sisters.

Down. – 1, Patient; 2, Refused; 3, Antonines; 4, End up; 5, Turn out; 6, America; 7, Working model; 10, Steel oneself; 15, Goalposts; 17, Lucerne; 18, Naïveté; 19, Strange; 20, Dairies; 22, Gusts.

No. 31

Across. – 1, Upper class; 6, Opus; 9, Amusing act; 10, Boom; 13, Distant; 15, Acumen; 16, Done in; 17, Stand no nonsense; 18, Nieces; 20, Allude; 21, Tethers; 22, Oyes; 25, Fire-raiser; 26, Tugs; 27, Kettledrum.

Down. – 1, Udal; 2, Plug; 3, Raisin; 4, Light punishment; 5, Second; 7, Proper noun; 8, Simon Peter; 11, Passing out; 12, Curate's egg; 13, Dead-set; 14, Tonsils; 19, Senile; 20, Arcade; 23, User; 24, Arum.

No. 32

Across. – 1, Clangour; 5, States; 9, Likewise; 10, Savory; 11, Marginal; 12, Chalet; 14, Skyscraper; 18, Peripheral; 22, Titian; 23, Get about; 24, Earthy; 25, Butter up; 26, Sparse; 27, Eye to eye.

Down. – 1, Column; 2, Askari; 3, Gawain; 4, Unshackled; 6, Teachers; 7, Trollope; 8, Shysters; 13, Estate duty; 15, Spatters; 16, Pretoria; 17, Splashes; 19, Past it; 20, Course; 21, Staple.

No. 33

Across. – 1, Godiva; 4, New pupil; 9, Enamel; 10, Assailed; 12, Noon; 13, Stays; 14, Mile; 17, Lodging-house; 20, Double vision; 23, Aged; 24, Ostia; 25, Mesh; 28, Nightjar; 29, Angora; 30, The Fates; 31, Beadle.

Down. – 1, Greenfly; 2, Diamonds; 3, View; 5, Essays of Elia; 6, Play; 7, Pulpit; 8, Ladled; 11, Stage by stage; 15, Pilot; 16, Aspic; 18, Side-road; 19, Inchoate; 21, Barnet; 22, Beagle; 26, Etna; 27, Ante.

No. 34

Across. – 1, Chatterboxes; 8, Usurper; 9, Unearth; 11, Goliath; 12, Sun-dial; 13, Asses; 14, Old scores; 16, Asparagus; 19, Ralph; 21, Ascribe; 23, Arsenal; 24, Mousers; 25, Actaeon; 26, Heated retort.

Down. – 1, Couples; 2, Appears; 3, Torch-song; 4, Roués; 5, Oceanic; 6, Earlier; 7, Burglar alarm; 10, Holds the line; 15, Disparate; 17, Picture; 18, Raiment; 19, Risotto; 20, Lenient; 22, Eased.

No. 35

Across. – 1, Babe; 3, Acorn; 6, Scar; 11, Look out; 12, Uplying; 13, Short and sweet; 16, Arrests; 17, Partner; 18, Cabaret; 21, Test Act; 23, Presentiments; 26, Charred; 27, Secrete; 28, Sake; 29, Onset; 30, Used.

Down. – 1, Ball; 2, Brother; 4, Cutlass; 5, Round up; 7, Crimean; 8, Rugs; 9, Tourist resort; 10, Flowery speech; 14, Match; 15, Crate; 19, Barrack; 20, Tuned in; 21, Trieste; 22, Anthems; 24, Acts; 25, Dead.

No. 36

Across. – 1, Pronouncement; 10, Poniard; 11, Stretch; 12, Rook; 13, Civil; 14, Blue; 17, Tarring; 18, Nomadic; 19, Outlast; 22, Butcher; 24, Slat; 25, Demon; 26, Dive; 29, Long-off; 30, Glimpse; 31, Cross-hatching.

Down. – 2, Rancour; 3, Noah; 4, Undoing; 5, Caspian; 6, More; 7, Nettled; 8, Spirits of salt; 9, Three-cornered; 15, Divan; 16, Smith; 20, Trainer; 21, Twelfth; 22, Brought; 23, Hairpin; 27, Toss; 28, With.

No. 37

Across. – 1, Slack season; 8, Score-boards; 11, Puck; 12, Side; 13, Lorient; 15, Orlando; 16, Soppy; 17, Coda; 18, Flat; 19, Grail; 21, Tethers; 22, Coterie; 23, Offa; 26, Lace; 27, French fried; 28, Passing whim.

Down. – 2, Lick; 3, Cartons; 4, Subs; 5, Amatory; 6, Odds; 7, Application; 8, Scared stiff; 9, Simnel-bread; 10, Demosthenes; 14, Tours; 15, Optic; 19, Grounds; 20, Lowbrow; 24, Aria; 25, When; 26, Levi.

No. 38

Across. – 1, There; 4, Simpleton; 8, America; 9, Batting; 10, Nags; 11, Obols; 12, Eggs; 15, Dental surgeon; 17, Dandie Dinmont; 20, Kind; 21, Niobe; 22, Tier; 25, Emulate; 26, Alecost; 27, Schooners; 28, Friar.

Down. – 1, Trainband; 2, Emerged; 3, Emit; 4, Starboard side; 5, Lute; 6, Tringle; 7, Negus; 9, Bulls and bears; 13, Anvil; 14, Brood; 16, Numerator; 18, Nonsuch; 19, Tripoli; 20, Keeps; 23, Halo; 24, Pelf.

No. 39

Across. – 1, Hatch; 4, Wandering; 9, Patball; 11, Touring; 12, Tang; 13, Acute; 14, Wail; 17, Ticket of leave; 19, Polite fiction; 21, Bait; 22, Reins; 23, Stow; 26, Officer; 27, Younger; 28, Hill towns; 29, Burns.

Down. – 1, Hepatitis; 2, Titanic; 3, Heat; 5, Not at all funny; 6, Emus; 7, Imitate; 8, Gogol; 10, Luck of the draw; 15, Celle; 16, March; 18, Sandworms; 19, Painful; 20, Integer; 21, Broth; 24, Scot; 25, Curb.

No. 40

Across. – 1, Wattage; 5, Call; 9, Private soldiers; 10, Oaks; 11, Corps; 12, Boil; 15, Tending; 16, Resided; 17, Drive up; 19, Teacher; 21, So on; 22, Smart; 23, Gust; 26, Pleasant weather; 27, Hero; 28, Nemesis.

Down. – 1, Wipe out; 2, Thinking it over; 3, Ajar; 4, Ere long; 5, Chopper; 6, Lady; 7, Bustled; 8, Second thoughts; 13, Files; 14, Asian; 17, Dust-pan; 18, Pimento; 19, Throw-in; 20, Retorts; 24, Esse; 25, Farm.

No. 41

Across. – 1, Holding forth; 8, Necktie; 9, Imprint; 11, Anaemia; 12, Erector; 13, Drear; 14, Drop-scene; 16, Saccharin; 19, Staff; 21, Enlarge; 23, Mullock; 24, Triplet; 25, Nankeen; 26, Winding-sheet.

Down. – 1, Hectare; 2, Latimer; 3, Icelander; 4, Grime; 5, Oppress; 6, Thistle; 7, Incandescent; 10, Three of a kind; 15, Ornaments; 17, Cellini; 18, Hurdled; 19, Silence; 20, Above it; 22, Eaten.

No. 42

Across. – 1, Lost Horizon; 9, Bill; 10, Symmetrical; 11, Heed; 14, Cheroot; 16, Praetor; 17, Kerry; 18, Otto; 19, Etui; 20, Weans; 22, Leaflet; 23, Tiepolo; 24, Auks; 28, Church bells; 29, Gang; 30, Dylan Thomas.

Down. – 2, Onyx; 3, Tame; 4, Outlook; 5, Ibis; 6, Oratory; 7, Fire station; 8, Glider pilot; 12, School badge; 13, Sent packing; 15, Tenet; 16, Print; 20, Weighty; 21, Silk-hat; 25, Area; 26, Hero; 27, Flea.

No. 43

Across. – 6, Probabilities; 8, Clever; 9, Lanterns; 10, Ire; 11, Pearls; 12, Travesty; 14, Uttered; 16, The Bomb; 20, Prompter; 23, Rating; 24, Ova; 25, Surmount; 26, Look on; 27, Hunger-strikes.

Down. – 1, Converse; 2, Fair Isle; 3, Billets; 4, Sienna; 5, Misère; 6, Pulled through; 7, Sanctimonious; 13, Vie; 15, RIP; 17, Heraldry; 18, Buttocks; 19, Protest; 21, Moment; 22, Truces.

No. 44

Across. – 1, Tutorship; 9, Aye-aye; 10, Appliance; 11, Bridge; 12, Lilac Time; 13, Aflame; 17, Eta; 19, Railway accident; 20, Exe; 21, Excuse; 25, Death-trap; 26, Ape man; 27, Bagatelle; 28, Canopy; 29, Adversely.

Down. – 2, Unpaid; 3, Oilman; 4, Shanty; 5, Income tax demand; 6, Hydrofoil; 7, Hard-baked; 8, Tenements; 14, Free-lance; 15, Miscreant; 16, Swiss Alps; 17, Eye; 18, Ace; 22, Strafe; 23, Otters; 24, Fallal.

No. 45

Across. – 1, Comprehended; 8, Rameses; 9, Satsuma; 11, Forlorn; 12, Scandal; 13, Lucid; 14, Angle-iron; 16, On a charge; 19, Joeys; 21, Growler; 23, Tintern; 24, Reawake; 25, Emperor; 26, Goalless draw.

Down. – 1, Cambric; 2, Mastoid; 3, Rising air; 4, Hosts; 5, Nut-case; 6, Ecuador; 7, Artful Dodger; 10, All and sundry; 15, Greatness; 17, Avocado; 18, Hold-all; 19, Juniper; 20, Eyebrow; 22, Reeve.

No. 46

Across. – 1, Backgammon; 6, Club; 10, Ruler; 11, Seed-pearl; 12, Fine arts; 13, Theme; 15, Dietary; 17, Alarmed; 19, Nostril; 21, Mahouts; 22, Motto; 24, Torrents; 27, Eccentric; 28, Get on; 29, Sash; 30, Inveterate.

Down. – 1, Bird; 2, Callipers; 3, Gorge; 4, Miserly; 5, Open sea; 7, Leave; 8, Balderdash; 9, Spot cash; 14, Odd numbers; 16, Airborne; 18, Mount Etna; 20, Lateran; 21, Miracle; 23, Ticks; 25, Eagle; 26, Once.

No. 47

Across. – 1, Terrapin; 5, Presto; 9, Aspirate; 10, Charge; 11, Cherries; 12, Barsac; 14, Air hostess; 18, Motionless; 22, Roller; 23, Aptitude; 24, Viable; 25, Revenant; 26, Detest; 27, Decadent.

Down. – 1, Thatch; 2, Rapier; 3 and 17, Aurora borealis; 4, In the field; 6, Rehearse; 7, Stressed; 8, Overcast; 13, Chess piece; 15, Improved; 16, Stalwart; 17, See 3 down; 19, Cinema; 20, Butane; 21, Beat it.

No. 48

Across. – 1, Fair and square; 10, Recruit; 11, Decline; 12, Unit; 13, Aback; 14, Mail; 17, Honesty; 18, Raiment; 19, Sultana; 22, Lozenge; 24, Ogre; 25, Whigs; 26, Amid; 29, Almoner; 30, Tannery; 31, Prisoners' base.

Down. – 2, Auction; 3, Rout; 4, Notably; 5, Sidecar; 6, Unco; 7, Reigate; 8, Draughtswoman; 9, Red-letter days; 15, Isaac; 16, Dizzy; 20, Lorimer; 21, Acheron; 22, Lighter; 23, Numbers; 27, Ends; 28, Snob.

No. 49

Across. – 1, Secret treaty; 8, Overset; 9, Sheriff; 11, Gallery; 12, Shallot; 13, Wides; 14, On a charge; 16, Acclaimed; 19, Salic; 21, Harrier; 23, Templar; 24, Reading; 25, Outrage, 26, Desert island.

Down. – 1, Shelled; 2, Cashews; 3, Entry form; 4, Tests; 5, Eyewash; 6, Trifler; 7, Foggy weather; 10, Fitted carpet; 15, Auditions; 17, Carnage; 18, Aniline; 19, Sumatra; 20, Lollard; 22, Right.

No. 50

Across. – 1, Back out; 5, Pile; 9, Sentence of death; 10, Mate; 11, Withy; 12, Char; 15, Nonplus; 16, Tea-tray; 17, Thinker; 19, Trained; 21, Iron; 22, Pleat; 23, Swan; 26, Bullet-proof vest; 27, Flee; 28, Marbled.

Down. – 1, Best man; 2, Constantinople; 3, Ones; 4, Tactics; 5, Prophet; 6, Lode; 7, Ash-tray; 8, Catherine-wheel; 13, Fluke; 14, Pagan; 17, Thimble; 18, Relapse; 19, Tea-room; 20, Denoted; 24, Tell; 25, Afar.

No. 51

Across. – 1, Cast off; 5, Tripped; 9, Procrastination; 10, Take; 11, Miami; 12, Beta; 15, Leasing; 16, Romance; 17, Cadence; 19, Trained; 21, Ache; 22, Ammon; 23, Isle; 26, Merchant bankers; 27, Disband; 28, Echidna.

Down. – 1, Capital; 2, Stocks and shares; 3, Oars; 4, Fasting; 5, Trimmer; 6, Iran; 7, Price on one's head; 8, Dentate; 13, Diana; 14, Smear; 17, Charmed; 18, Ermined; 19, Trouble; 20, Deep sea; 24, Thea; 25, Inch.

No. 52

Across. – 1, Headlight; 9, Delete; 10, Outsiders; 11, Hisses; 12, Strong men; 13, Robust; 17, The; 19, Collision course; 20, Wed; 21, Powwow; 25, Lazy-tongs; 26, Inured; 27, Unspotted; 28, Abides; 29, Strappado.

Down. – 2, Equity; 3, Despot; 4, Indigo; 5, Horseshoe magnet; 6, Semicolon; 7, Set square; 8, Bed-sitter; 14, Sceptical; 15, Slow music; 16, Disobeyed; 17, Tiw; 18, End; 22, Myopia; 23, Hot tip; 24, Agreed.

No. 53

Across. – 1, Sheriffs; 5, Silage; 9 and 10, American accent; 12, Test match; 13, Grill; 14, Chic; 16, Naïveté; 19, Too late; 21, Moon; 24, Musty; 25, Perchance; 27, Onager; 28, Multiple; 29, Basalt; 30, By George.

Down. – 1, Shanty; 2, Even so; 3, Idiom; 4, Frantic; 6, Incognito; 7, Alewives; 8, Extolled; 11, Shan; 15, Heavy meal; 17, Atom bomb; 18, Bobstays; 20, Espy; 21, Mercury; 22, Sniper; 23, Revere; 26, Hythe.

No. 54

Across. – 6, Press-cuttings; 8, Visage; 9, Go to town; 10, Sue; 11, Etches; 12, Overdone; 14, Traders; 16, May-time; 20, Redgrave; 23, Horace; 24, Nil; 25, Protract; 26, Emilia; 27, Rough estimate.

Down. – 1, Rehashed; 2, Assessor; 3, Burgeon; 4, Statue; 5, United; 6, Printer's error; 7, Sewing-machine; 13, Ray; 15, Err; 17, Athletic; 18, Terminal; 19, Dentist; 21, Get out; 22, Apache.

No. 55

Across. – 1, Reign; 4, Insurance; 9, Nettles; 11, Confine; 12, Tong; 13, Canny; 14, Chat; 17, Feel off-colour; 19, Work of fiction; 21, Fare; 22, Pluck; 23, Game; 26, Meeting; 27, Reefers; 28, Dismissed; 29, Mason.

Down. – 1, Runs to fat; 2, Intense; 3, Nile; 5, Second officer; 6, Ring; 7, Neither; 8, Exeat; 10, Staff colleges; 15, Tours; 16, Tosca; 18, Hangers-on; 19, Wardens; 20, In a mess; 21, Famed; 24, Fifi; 25, Beam.

No. 56

Across. – 1, Complete; 5, Sprout; 9, Rock-cake; 10, Used up; 11, One-class; 12, Spirit; 14, Better half; 18, Chesterton; 22, Osprey; 23, Agnostic; 24, Dressy; 25, Forenoon; 26, Dating; 27, Eminence.

Down. – 1, Carton; 2, Mocked; 3, Locals; 4, Takes heart; 6, Passport; 7, Old dream; 8, Tipstaff; 13, Strong-room; 15, Accorded; 16, Help-meet; 17, Utterson; 19, Modern; 20, Strown; 21, Sconce.

No. 57

Across. – 8, Old Norse; 9, Headed; 10, Ria; 11, Hold over; 12, Nooses; 13, Repent at leisure; 15, Precept; 18, Migrate; 21, Mountain resorts; 24, Script; 25, Antedate; 26, Its; 27, Mosaic; 28, Tropical.

Down. – 1, Alcove; 2, On edge; 3, Private practice; 4, Serrate; 5, Change direction; 6, Carouser; 7, Sewer-rat; 14, Pie; 16, Root-crop; 17, Cannibal; 19, Ayr; 20, In haste; 22, Ordain; 23, Titian.

No. 58

Across. – 1, Narrating; 9, Gobang; 10, Dexterity; 11, Stater; 12, Australia; 13, Boring; 17, Egg; 19, Infidel; 20, Insight; 21, Fin; 23, Option; 27, Idle hands; 28, Seesaw; 29, Expending; 30, Needed; 31, Edelweiss.

Down. – 2, Avenue; 3, Rotate; 4, Tarmac; 5, Nothing; 6, Boat-house; 7, Partridge; 8, Aggregate; 14, Limousine; 15, Off the peg; 16, Advocates; 17, Elf; 18, Gin; 22, Indexed; 24, Befell; 25, Candle; 26, Adonis.

No. 59

Across. – 1, Measure out; 8, Useful; 9, Dutch treat; 10, Oracle; 11, Love-letter; 12, Inlets; 13, Hewn; 15, Grantee; 19, Aground; 21, X-ray; 22, Acacia; 25, Make-up room; 27, Revamp; 28, Labour pool; 29, Dragée; 30, Seventh day.

Down. – 1, Middling; 2, Active; 3, Up-hill; 4, Egret; 5, Tutoring; 6, Seraglio; 7, Bulletin; 13, Her; 14, Way; 16, Rocketry; 17, No change; 18, Examples; 20, Dismally; 23, Spirit; 24, No good; 26, Erode.

No. 60

Across. – 1, Diction; 5, Oval; 9, Straightforward; 10, Easy; 11, Spoon; 12, Ogle; 15, Drifter; 16, Matched; 17, Tenders; 19, Pelican; 21, Drag; 22, Faint; 23, Band; 26, One over the eight; 27, Snow; 28, Debased.

Down. – 1, Distend; 2, Christian names; 3, Iris; 4, No-hoper; 5, Off form; 6, Airs; 7, Red lead; 8, Rang the changes; 13, Other; 14, Style; 17, Tedious; 18, Sparrow; 19, Pinched; 20, Nodated; 24, Oven; 25, Herb.

No. 61

Across. – 1, Hot favourite; 8, Largish; 9, Regrets; 11, Bandeau; 12, Calomel; 13, Outré; 14, The masses; 16, Estaminet; 19, Poser; 21, Handsaw; 23, Martini; 24, Regular; 25, Orlando; 26, Landed gentry.

Down. – 1, Hard nut; 2, Trireme; 3, Ashburton; 4, Osric; 5, Regalia; 6, Thermos; 7, Club together; 10, Sole survivor; 15, Extempore; 17, Tanagra; 18, Muscled; 19, Partlet; 20, Spinney; 22, World.

No. 62

Across. – 1, Agitators; 9, Primate; 10, Adheres; 11, Average; 12, Man and boy; 14, Psalmist; 15, Weekly; 17, Ospreys; 20, Assets; 23, Dealt out; 25, Tethering; 26, Transit; 27, Mimicry; 28, Crammer; 29, Stage-name.

Down. – 2 and 3, God save the mark; 4, Tuesdays; 5, Splays; 6, Wine-glass; 7, Samaria; 8, Deserters; 13, Operate; 15, Woodstock; 16, Loathsome; 18, Yachting; 19, Faraday; 21, Serbian; 22, Tantrum; 24, Utters.

No. 63

Across. – 1, Babel; 4, Short-leg; 10, Channel; 11, Learned; 12, Arab; 13, Scoop; 14, Wary; 17, Hell for leather; 19, Correct bearing; 22, Chin; 23, Level; 24, Fist; 27, Whippet; 28, Tourist; 29, Dressers; 30, Paled.

Down. – 1, Backache; 2, Bradawl; 3, Lent; 5, Hold one's breath; 6, Roam; 7, Lineage; 8, Giddy; 9, Electric heater; 15, Afore; 16, Strap; 18, Agitated; 20, Orifice; 21, Initial; 22, Cowed; 25, Spas; 26, Dump.

No. 64

Across. – 1, No time to lose; 8, Patents; 9, Linctus; 11, Olivier; 12, Plainer; 13, Ingle; 14, Buttercup; 16. Ebullient; 19, Casca; 21, Imports; 23, Earnest; 24, Earshot; 25, Allegro; 26, Estrangement.

Down. – 1, Netting; 2, Tin mine; 3, Miserable; 4, Tulip; 5, Lineage; 6, Satanic; 7, Opposite side; 10, Strip cartoon; 15, Title-page; 17, Umpires; 18, Lurcher; 19, Coralie; 20, Sleight; 22, Sit-in.

No. 65

Across. – 6, Discharged; 8, Chum; 9, Mad hatter; 11, Note; 12, Tot; 13, Peasantry; 16, Room; 17, Applaud; 18, Cool off; 20, Fret; 21, Breakdown; 23, Mar; 24, Cone; 25, Addressee; 29, Best; 30, Effrontery.

Down. – 1, Firm; 2, Acid; 3, Mama; 4, Agitate; 5, Just for fun; 7, Dirty work; 8, Contralto; 10, His; 13, Paper money; 14, Allotment; 15, Adumbrate; 19, Head off; 22, Dis; 26, Enow; 27, Site; 28, Eire.

No. 66

Across. – 7, Mounts Bay; 8, Nanny; 10, Put in for; 11, Cringe; 12, Near; 13, Go too far; 15, Isolate; 17, Reverie; 20, Get about; 22, Test; 25, Withal; 26, At a price; 27, Skins; 28, Low comedy.

Down. – 1, Rogue; 2, On fire; 3, Ask for it; 4, Barrage; 5, Baritone; 6, Enigmatic; 9, Scot; 14, Asterisks; 16, Leashing; 18, Entrance; 19, Attaboy; 21, Oils; 23, Scrimp; 24, Acids.

No. 67

Across. – 1, Banbury Cross; 9, Abettor; 10, Realist; 11, Lido; 12, Again; 13, Turn; 16, Acrobat; 17, Termini; 18, Enchant; 21, Ripping; 23, Tide; 24, Jemmy; 25, Fair; 28, Recline; 29, Leonine; 30, Alice Springs.

Down. – 1, Blender; 2, Nato; 3, Upright; 4, Yorkist; 5, Real; 6, Stimuli; 7 and 8, Parliamentary standing order; 14, Obeah; 15, Props; 19, Codicil; 20, Theseus; 21, Rambler; 22, Italics; 26, Disc; 27, Down.

No. 68

Across. – 1, Cold fish; 5, Escort; 9, Push-over; 10, Camera; 11, Overripe; 12, Scales; 14, Street lamp; 18, Pace-makers; 22, Rotary; 23, Accusers; 24, Tramps; 25, Distance; 26, Riders; 27, Indolent.

Down. – 1, Captor; 2, Lashed; 3, Floury; 4, Sweepstake; 6, Staccato; 7, Overload; 8, Transept; 13, Detraction; 15, Operator; 16, Scotland; 17, Improper; 19, Just so; 20, Seance; 21, Assert.

No. 69

Across. – 1, Hearth; 4, Sparkled; 9, Number; 10, Misstate; 12, Band; 13, Axles; 14, Beam; 17, Little office; 20, Distilleries; 23, Leek; 24, Pouch; 25, Levi; 28, Motor-car; 29, Common; 30, Sadducee; 31, Banned.

Down. – 1, Handbill; 2, Ammonite; 3, Tied; 5, Pride of place; 6, Rise; 7, Leader; 8, Dreams; 11, Extortionate; 15, Slain; 16, Screw; 18, Linesman; 19, Assigned; 21, Climbs; 22, Wetted; 26, Urdu; 27, Coma.

No. 70

Across. – 8, Da capo; 9, Pleasing; 10, Stills; 11, Rhodesia; 12, Eat; 13, Come on; 14, Attended; 16, Studded; 18, Prelate; 23, Brandish; 27, Orford; 28, Arm; 29, Romantic; 30, Maoist; 31, Biblical; 32, Tie-pin.

Down. – 1, Last post; 2, Wallsend; 3, Nonsense; 4, Spartan; 5, Get out; 6, Astern; 7, In time; 15, Eve; 17, Dud; 19, Room-mate; 20, Left over; 21, Turnspit; 22, Shackle; 24, Rookie; 25, Nearly; 26, Intact.

No. 71

Across. – 1, World atlas; 6, Pays; 9, Fritillary; 10, Saga; 13, Leashed; 15, Author; 16, Nereid; 17, Landscape artist; 18, Trains; 20, Scrawl; 21, Seasick; 22, Eton; 25, Single fare; 26, Tiff; 27, Lasting out.

Down. – 1, Wife; 2, Rail; 3, Driver; 4, Telescopic sight; 5, Airmen; 7, Academical; 8, Standstill; 11, Wall Street; 12, Stand aloof; 13, Loosens; 14, Derrick; 19, Selina; 20, Screen; 23, Cato; 24, Feet.

No. 72

Across. – 6, No love lost; 8, Hind; 9, Toscanini; 11, Peep; 12, Lie; 13, Post-natal; 16, Rede; 17, Rejoice; 18, Potomac; 20, Beat; 21, Monastery; 23, Ham; 24, Asia; 25, Exercises; 29, Plod; 30, Thirty-nine.

Down. – 1, Colt; 2, Bows; 3, Beta; 4, Goliath; 5, Incendiary; 7, Trillions; 8, Hyperbole; 10, Cut; 13, Prehensile; 14, Shorthand; 15, No comment; 19, Interim; 22, Tai; 26, City; 27 and 28, Sing Sing.

No. 73

Across. – 6, Match-box label; 8; Stupor; 9, Postcard; 10, Toe; 11, Fringe; 12, Resisted; 14, Hashish; 16, Haddock; 20, Gin and It; 23, Drawls; 24, Awe; 25, Statuary; 26, Resume; 27, Caught in a trap.

Down. – 1, At a pinch; 2, Shortens; 3, Compère; 4, Clasps; 5, Abacus; 6, Materialistic; 7, Large-scale map; 13, Ind; 15, Inn; 17, Alderman; 18, Dear Sirs; 19, Stays in; 21, Arthur; 22, Drachm.

No. 74

Across. – 1, Desert rat; 9, Raiment; 10, Chaplet; 11, Natalie; 12, Quartered; 14, By the way; 15, Stereo; 17, Printer; 20, Sea-god; 23, Overcast; 25, Perimeter; 26, Diverse; 27, Pagodas; 28, Red Hand; 29, Sedentary.

Down. – 2, Exhaust; 3, Emperor; 4, Therefor; 5, Trendy; 6, Wiltshire; 7, Bellows; 8, Steelyard; 13, Ebonite; 15, Secondary; 16, Epicurean; 18, Estimate; 19, Pervade; 21, Alecost; 22, Open air; 24, Spends.

No. 75

Across. – 1, Type; 3, Paste; 6, Afar; 11, Confuse; 12, Pink gin; 13, Undergraduate; 16, Creased; 17, Twosome; 18, Reactor; 21, Padlock; 23, Heart-sickness; 26, Borstal; 27, Lateran; 28, Node; 29, Bandy; 30, Hemp.

Down. – 1, Tuck; 2, Penance; 4, Avenged; 5, Topmast; 7, Fagotto; 8, Ring; 9, Supersaturate; 10, Insubordinate; 14, Score; 15, Berks; 19, Averred; 20, Rosella; 21, Pickled; 22, Observe; 24, Oban; 25, Snap.

No. 76

Across. – 1, Deliberating; 8, Hornsea; 9, Stay put; 11, Lentisk; 12, Sincere; 13, Opens; 14, Where is it?; 16, Safety net; 19, Capon; 21, Awaited; 23, Meanest; 24, Titania; 25, Nattier; 26, Knock-out blow.

Down. – 1, Durance; 2, Lassies; 3, Black swan; 4, Rasps; 5, Trainee; 6, Napless; 7, The lion's part; 10, Treat in store; 15, Estaminet; 17, Flatten; 18, Titanic; 19, Chattel; 20, Preview; 22, Draco.

No. 77

Across. – 8, Set piece; 9, Hold up; 10, Doe; 11, Inventor; 12, Curate; 13, Sell one's country; 15, Captain; 18, Beheads; 21, Displaced person; 24, On tour; 25, Thoughts; 26, Obi; 27, Assets; 28, Oil-paint.

Down. – 1, Séance; 2, Appeal; 3, Getting it across; 4, Redress; 5, The chosen people; 6, Florence; 7, Muttered; 14, Lap; 16, Alienist; 17, Tips over; 19, Ass; 20, Mention; 22, Raglan; 23, Outing.

No. 78

Across. – 1, Comatose; 5, Spited; 9, Separate; 10, Glared; 11, Round off; 12, Asleep; 14, Second home; 18, Contention; 22, U-boats; 23, Maudling; 24, Armlet; 25, Division; 26, Enlist; 27, Snuggery.

Down. – 1, Castro; 2, Map out; 3, Tirade; 4, Set of teeth; 6, Palisade; 7, Turned on; 8, Didapper; 13, Coloration; 15, Accurate; 16, Informal; 17, Heathens; 19, Idling; 20, Finite; 21, Agency.

No. 79

Across. – 3, Facts; 8 and 9, Casual labour; 10, Hallam; 11, Regroups; 12, Bye; 13, Castle; 14, Nota bene; 17 and 19, Keep out of sight; 23, Saratoga; 27, Oberon; 29, Sir; 30, Admonish; 31, Etudes; 32, Clothe; 33, Cutter; 34, Range.

Down. – 1, Banana; 2, Full stop; 3, Flambeau; 4 and 22, Current fashion; 5, Slight; 6, Absorb; 7, Turpin; 13 and 24, Cakes and ale; 15, Ass; 16, Eaten; 18, Opt; 20, Florence; 21, Inequity; 22, See 4 down; 24, See 13 down; 25, Adopts; 26, Oliver; 28, Ox-eyed.

No. 80

Across. – 8, Here; 9, Ham; 10, Hotbed; 11, Malign; 12, Insulate; 13, See the funny side; 15, Take off; 17, Bridges; 20, Complete picture; 23, Deserted; 25, Billed; 26, Chaste; 27, Wow; 28, Nous.

Down. – 1, Debate; 2, Belittle; 3, Change of weather; 4, Impious; 5, Chasing rainbows; 6, Stilts; 7, Felt; 14, Die; 16, Ago; 18, Dateline; 19, Let down; 21, Please; 22, Rhesus; 24, Echo.

MORE ABOUT PENGUINS, PELICANS AND PUFFINS

For further information about books available from Penguins please write to Dept EP, Penguin Books Ltd, Harmondsworth, Middlesex UB7 0DA.

In the U.S.A.: For a complete list of books available from Penguins in the United States write to Dept DG, Penguin Books, 299 Murray Hill Parkway, East Rutherford, New Jersey 07073.

In Canada: For a complete list of books available from Penguins in Canada write to Penguin Books Canada Ltd, 2801 John Street, Markham, Ontario L3R 1B4.

In Australia: For a complete list of books available from Penguins in Australia write to the Marketing Department, Penguin Books Australia Ltd, P.O. Box 257, Ringwood, Victoria 3134.

In New Zealand: For a complete list of books available from Penguins in New Zealand write to the Marketing Department, Penguin Books (N.Z.) Ltd, Private Bag, Takapuna, Auckland 9.

In India: For a complete list of books available from Penguins in India write to Penguin Overseas Ltd, 706 Eros Apartments, 56 Nehru Place, New Delhi 110019.

TANGRAM
The Ancient Chinese Shapes Game
Joost Elffers

Tangram, the 1000-year-old Chinese puzzle, is an exciting game which stimulates creativity and fantasy, and which can be played by one person or by a group.

The game consists of seven pieces, formed by cutting a square in a certain way, with which you can copy the examples given in this book. This may sound easy – but try it.

THE PENGUIN BOOK OF MAZES
60 beautiful and beastly labyrinths with solutions
Rolf Myller

There are three sets of mazes in this book, and they all look the same. But beware – because each one has a different solution.

Collect your pencil and patience, and you can set off from start to finish – or from finish to start, it doesn't really matter. But playing mazes should be fun, so if you get too frustrated look at the solutions at the back. Who knows, you might even find one the author missed!

THE MOSCOW PUZZLES
Boris A. Kordemsky

A man has to row a wolf, a goat and some cabbage across a river in a boat which will only hold himself and one of the three. If he leaves them alone, the wolf will eat the goat and the goat will eat the cabbage. How does he get them across?

These and dozens of other problems in arithmetic, algebra, geometry, logic and common sense appear in this collection, which has been a best-seller in Russia for several years and is already regarded as *the* classic puzzle book.

THE PENGUIN BOOK OF CARD GAMES
David Parlett

From conventional Bridge and Poker to Klabberjass, Spite and
Malice, Schafkopf and Bassadewitz, the 300 games are arranged in
related groups, with an introduction to the pedigree and peculiarities
of each family. More than seventy are described in detail, with hints
on strategy and tricky points, while another 200 are concisely
explained.

THE PENGUIN BOOK OF PATIENCE
David Parlett

Playing a game of patience is the mental equivalent of jogging – it
tones the brain up nicely and banishes mental flabbiness.

A companion to the *Penguin Book of Card Games*, David Parlett's
entertaining and original collection of patience games is the first for
nearly a century.

The author has adopted a systematic approach designed to suit every
mood and temperament, and has arranged the games into three
categories: first, those which require care and patience; second, those
requiring balance of judgement and card sense; third, those which call for
the type of positional analysis more usually associated with chess
problems than card games.

BRIDGE
Terence Reese

In this complete and objective account of the modern game of bridge, the
reader is assumed to possess outline knowledge of the mechanics of
the game and is then taken through the fundamental principles of
bidding and play up to a fairly advanced level of strategy. Moreover,
like most modern teachers who tell a player that having so many
s he must bid such-and-such, Terence Reese treats the reader as
elligent being, carries him along at a fair rate and gives him
hance to develop his card sense.